CAPTURE CLIENTS
CLOSE DEALS

A **SIMPLE** WAY TO GAIN CLIENTS
WITHOUT CONVINCING OR CHASING

STEVE NAPOLITAN

CAPTURE CLIENTS CLOSE DEALS
A Simple Way to Gain Clients Without Convincing or Chasing

Published by: Bestseller Big Business Publishing
Manufactured in the United States of America

Cover design by: Colby Shaules
Content Editing: Jon Low, Kelly Thomas & Trevor Crane
Book Bonuses: Steve Napolitan & The Now Academy

For more information about Steve Napolitan or to book him for your next event or media interview, please visit: http://www.stevenapolitan.com/speaking/

DEDICATION

I want to dedicate *Capture Clients Close Deals* to all those that **guided** me to become the man I am today, and to all those that continue to light the path for my **continued growth**.

My Parents: who encouraged me to follow my heart—I learned many lessons from you. The biggest lesson, one from my Dad, has been work ethic and commitment, from my Mom—to be able to approach and talk with anyone. Without you, I would not be alive.

Carlos Aparicio: who trained me at my job while I was in college. You showed me how to run a side business—I worked the phones, at every break and every lunch, to get my first business up and running Without you, I would not have started my first company.

David Trifeletti: my cousin, you were my early mentor on sales. Without you, I wouldn't have advanced to bigger deals.

Jeffery Slayter: my main coach and mentor, you taught me how to stop working hard, start working smarter, and enjoy my life. Without you, I would not have the freedom I have now.

Tommy Voris: who taught me to focus. Without you, I would still be averagely doing several things, instead of doing things great, one at a time.

Michelle Masters: my mindset coach, you helped me add new behaviors into my life—allowing me to have what I want even when my subconscious was saying "No." Without you, I would still be sabotaging my life.

Carl Buchheit: who taught Jeffery and Michelle—you have taught me how to honor what is, and to fully embrace what can be. Without you, I would not have had the help form Jeffery and Michelle, and I would not be taking my life to even more powerful places.

Trevor Crane and Jon Low: who helped me, every step of the way, to make this book happen. Without them, this book would not be in your hands.

My wife Jen and my amazing children: who love and support me in the good times, and the bad times, and see my potential—even when I do not. Without you, my life would have a much smaller purpose, and my #1 job title would be lost… "Father."

To all the above-mentioned and the many people not (mentioned)—it would take another book to mention everyone— I have **so much love** and **gratitude** for you all. **Thank you**.

———————————————————

Here are some additional gifts (for you) to help you get the most out of this book: CaptureClientsCloseDeals.com/bonuses

PREFACE

I was a slave to the business that was meant to give me freedom. I was overweight, and depressed. I'd lost sight of my vision. I was working hard, in my business, to make a living. But, little did I know, that working hard was *consuming* my opportunity to enjoy my life. I'm talking about working so hard, that, sometimes, I would eat one meal a day, because I didn't want to stop. I'd grab something quick, and it usually was not healthy. These unhealthy eating habits lead to me gaining **over 80lbs**. And, coupled with my overwhelming stress of not being happy with the lifestyle my businesses demanded, I started to breakdown. I started to question if I would ever be a good enough businessman. My life had become the exact opposite of what I had originally envisioned—I was not living the lifestyle of a successful, happy, entrepreneur.

I come from a hard working Italian family—growing up, my dad worked *all the time*. So much so that when I went to bed at night, he would still be at work. While I was sleeping, he was awake, alert and doing his thing to provide for our family. I don't know how he did it for so many decades, but I'm grateful he did. He provided for our family. But when it came to college, it was up to us. My father didn't have the money to pay for our education, and the government denied us any financial aid for education because, apparently, dad *earned too much*. So I was stuck in a pickle, and did the best I could.

I was in college, working a 50+ hour week job, while studying, full-time, in film school. I had to pay for college fees. In film school, if you don't know what it's like, a students has to work on required film projects (on top of the standard classes). . This can take **hours and hours.** So, I would start my day, at 4a.m, by working my day shift so I could earn some cash to support myself. Then, at night, I'd go to film school, and work on all my projects till about 2 (in the morning!). After working myself to the *bone*, I would drag myself out of the studios to go on home—sometimes I'd have less than 2 hours sleep. And, by the time I fell asleep, I'd have to wake up and do it all again.

Maybe you can relate to my story? Maybe not. But, either way, my work and study obligations *ruled* my life. So, one day, I basically freaked out. After another long day of work, I looked in the mirror, and I saw my dad. Not just in the way I looked, but in the way I lived! I was getting up before sunrise, I was getting home after sunset. I was working while others were sleeping, and I was working (I am sure) even in my dreams. I *had* to break the pattern.

Eventually, I had what I thought was one of those light-bulb moments. "Why not start your own business? Earn more money, control your time, and do things *your way,* Steve?" That's what I told myself. I smiled at the thought, thinking it would be much easier. But, soon after starting my own business, I realized I *bought a more stressful* job. But this time, it wasn't a job I could leave. It was my baby. And I was working harder than ever. *I was working not to work.* What a joke. So, there I was, struggling to gain more clients, struggling to have a life.

The same pattern repeated itself when I went solo. I was ruled by two things: chasing clients and getting deals across the line. I was spending hours on end, chasing clients. With perseverance, this did work out. Almost one in every ten people I approached became clients. Problem was, I was spending an hour on every potential client, and, with travel time, that meant I was spending 40 hours of my life to get *one client*.

Does this sound like your typical approach to getting clients? Are you working hours and hours on end to secure a **single client**? Luckily for you, the principles and processes I share in this book will help you *capture clients* more efficiently (and with ease).By using the principles and processes—in *Capture Clients Close Deals*— you can spend *much* less time getting the client you want. Today, two out of three potential clients I approach become paying clients. That's a 66% reduction in time and effort (from my previous 40 hour/one client system)! If only I knew what I knew, but *back then*!

Most people who start their own business are great at *delivery*, but struggle to create and implement and effective marketing strategies. It's not something we are taught in school. It's not something most of us are taught in life. Like *ever*. But it is also the *oxygen* for any business that wants to grow **massively, healthily** and **sustainably**.

Is it hard to learn? No. It's harder *not* to learn. I've designed my approach (what I'm about to teach you) so the everyday human being can put it to work. As you now know, I didn't grow up privileged. I didn't have Albert Einstein's IQ. In fact, I was an artist—a filmmaker. The only thing that got me through was my willingness to learn and my ability to work hard, no matter how much things sucked. I'd always dust myself off after a few failures, and continue on.

That's why I shared my story with you. You don't need to be exceptionally talented or knowledgeable to implement what I'm about to share. You simply need to be willing to learn, willing to be coached, and willing to take consistent, effective, *action*. It'll save you the many years I spent trying to figure it out on my own.

Today, I don't have to stress out about gaining clients. I GET to choose the ones that I actually want to work with. If they aren't a match for my business, and the life I want, I politely and professionally say no. I want this empowering position for everyone. I want this for *you*. This (learning how to empower myself) is something I never got from my loving parents; I taught myself this crucial skill. And, now, I am able to teach it to my children. And I'm so grateful, because I'm sure my father would look at this and celebrate the fact that I found a way to have things be *better* for our family. For you, it could also mean having more time to travel the world, more peace of mind to pursue your hobbies, or a combination of everything.

Now, I map out what I want in my personal life and then design my business around that. I've been able to travel the world with my wife and three kids. We lived in Australia a few years back. As a family we've taken two big road trips—across the United States!

When my son was studying Thomas Edison, we went to southern Florida to visit his winter lab. He's now in love with comics, so we took the family to Comic-Con and my kids were able to meet Stan Lee, an Icon in the comic book industry and previous president of Marvel Comics. After we did this my son came to me and said, "Dad, thank you for taking me to Comic-Con. Most kids don't get to go to something like this, and you also paid more so I could meet Stan Lee. Thank you Dad."

I told him, "You're welcome and I'm so happy you are filled with such gratitude." This brings a tear to my eye, because my Dad was not able to do these things with me. Each year, I'm gaining more family time, while my businesses continue to grow. I'm not sharing this to brag, but more to tell you what is possible. In fact, that is why I wrote this book. I want to help as many people have the freedom they desire, while continuing to enjoy my own.

So it makes me wonder, how much will it change your life and business if you only have to do *a third* of the amount of work you are doing now? What will it mean for your life and business, when you can *capture* more clients, with greater ease and confidence? But, perhaps, the bigger question is—what if you can earn more money in your business, *and* have more time (i.e. more freedom) for other things in life too?

Think about it. It's important. In the coming chapters, I'm going to show you how to make this (earning more money while enjoying more freedom) a reality. How? We'll get to that soon, of course. But just know that there are many things you probably *don't know*. But, when brought to light, will make *the difference* you want for your business and life. And, I'll give you the small steps to make the things you know, but are not doing, for whatever reason, happen.

You see, in this book, I'm about to share with you the simplest and proven principles to grow your business with ease, to *Capture Clients* and *Close Deals*. And this book is also *much more* than just growing your business and fattening your bank account. At heart, it is about *regaining* your life. No one starts a business to be ruled *by* their business. We do it so we have *success* that we can enjoy, and success that we can feel *great* about. Something that makes you say, at the end of the day, "Wow! Going into business was *so* worth it! It is so fun!"

That's what you want, right? If not, you wouldn't be reading this book. Most likely, you want to grow a business that pays you well, that you enjoy, so you can have what you want in all areas of life. Otherwise, it (building your business) would *not* be worth it.

So, wherever you are in life or business, know there is a way to have more of what you want. Whether you just want more revenue, so you can pay yourself better and relax a little. Or, perhaps you want a system and process to manage the growing pains you are experiencing in your amazing business. Or maybe you are sick and tired of serving customers who are a drag, and want to work with people you'd actually *enjoy* seeing.

All my clients have experienced these issues. And, with simple tweaks—such as a *simple survey*, or changing *a few words* in their marketing collateral—they have *gained more customers* within a matter of days, opened multiple franchises within the year, or even reduced their cost of expensive advertising that simply *didn't work* like it was supposed to. And, the *best thing* about it—you don't have to convince, chase or *twist* someone's arm to make your customers buy what you have to offer.

So the focus of this book is *capturing* more clients and *closing* deals. It's fundamentally about business development. But it's about doing it right. It's about doing it from the heart. We will explore how you can:

- Find clients that you would love, absolutely *adore*, working with every day. It makes business fun and inspiring.

- Implement processes and ways to get more clients you love, with *less effort* and *less cost*.

- Build a business that supports your life. Not just the other way around.

That's why I created this book. It is a truly simple way to gain clients without convincing or chasing. It's a way to make sure the clients you work with are ones who inspire you, rather than expire you.

INTRODUCTION:

How to use this book!

Now, I've poured my all into this book. But it might not be good enough. Sadly. Want to know why?—because I can't *build your business* for you. I can help you. But you need to put **great effort** in too. It has to be a team approach. I can help you spot the gold, and give you the best shovel in the world. BUT, If you don't dig, if you do nothing, that's what you'll get— ,**nothing** (no change, no gold). SO, are you ready for **lasting, sustainable**, change? Yes? Good. Here goes:

This book is for you if:

1. You have a dream or desire for more money, more clients, more notoriety in your field, etc. or more positive, long-lasting, change,

2. You are willing to take action (otherwise, year after year will pass and you will be no closer to your dream or desire. And, yes, I did say "YEAR" after "YEAR"—don't wait— take action NOW!

3. You are coachable. You are willing to take what I share and apply it. If you keep doing it your way, you will keep having the same result.

You have to have ALL three. Otherwise, you should just put this book down, give it to someone else, or return it. I know this may sound harsh, but my intent is to help you **get results**. If you choose to read this book, please **play full out**. Take all the notes you can, do the exercises (**you can download the workbook accompaniment to this book at no charge here: CaptureClientsCloseDeals.com/bonuses**, and take action. If you do that—take action!—and follow the steps, **you will change your life and business forever.**

As you read *Capture Clients Close Deals*, you will notice that I share a lot about *mindset*. Here's the deal: **if you don't mind your mind, you can't mind your business**. Your thoughts create your reality, AND your business is part of your reality. Therefore, mind your thoughts—cultivate and pay attention to only those (thoughts) that serve you for the better—better thinking; better business. Here's one strategy that I've cultivated (and now practice) that has paid off **exponentially:** *stop selling* and *gain more* clients. This might seem *contradictory*. But that's part of the reason why it works; so, stay tuned, I'll share more about this strategy (later in the book). You will also notice, as you read, how many things *unrelated* to business, directly impact the success of your business—such as our capacity, as entrepreneurs, to understand and relate to human beings on levels deeper than their *best friends* even go. The secrets I share (in *Capture Clients Close Deals*) aren't known to most. In fact, many think they should be hidden from us. **But I want to share them with you**—if we don't pass the torch, we can't share the light.

You see, these same people that want to keep these lessons to themselves, believe there is a limited amount of resources in the world. I disagree. **We live in a universe with unlimited resources.** You can have **what you truly want**, and it doesn't mean someone else has to go without—we (everyone on the planet!) can have what we truly want—**abundance is unlimited.**

In *Capture Clients Close Deals*, I will teach you how to:

1. Simplify the process of gaining clients. Less stress, more time, and more returns.

2. Serve more people, while also growing your business (at the same time!).

3. Free yourself of nasty clients and only work with your perfect clients (what I call "Wow Clients.")

4. Stop guessing and start knowing what your clients want, with certainty.

5. Attract the perfect client, over and over again. You'll learn exactly what to say, so you can create an amazing client base, and generate *predictable* revenue.

6. Build trust and rapport with your client's deepest pain, and why this is **SO** important—99% of people (entrepreneurs?) avoid this crucial process. This is why their customers *forget* them.

7. Understand your client's deepest desires, beyond what they tell you they want, to find if they are a match for your

business. With this, your clients will feel like you have read their minds, and connected with their hearts.

8. Make offers with **confidence** and **ease**, AND hear the word YES more often (from the clients your really want).

9. Apply these skills, step-by-step, into your business and your life—so that you can succeed, with ease, at both! By the inch it is easy. By the mile it is *impossible*. Adding and changing things requires you to manage what is going on in your business *now*, so that you can begin to carve out a new path (for your business, for your life).

CONTENTS

PART FIVE
More People Buy To Get Rid Of Pain

PART SIX
Find Their Deepest Desire

PART SEVEN
Making The Offer Simple With Integrity

PART EIGHT
Taking Action

PART ONE

Stop Pitching
And Start Giving

CHAPTER 1

Sales Is About Giving

"You can have everything in life you want, if you just help enough other people get what they want."
—Zig Ziglar

Picture this—in your hands, you have a magic token that can change someone's life. Now, imagine yourself in the shoes of someone else. As they look at you, experience you, and receive your energy—what would it be like? Likely, they'll experience you as warm, caring, and wanting to serve. Now, picture another scenario—in your hands, you have a warrant to claim someone's property—maybe a house, or business (something he/she has worked hard to earn)—and, let's just say, you feel like exercising that warrant. What would it be like to be on the receiving end of that? Likely, you'd feel threatened—l like something is up. As if something *bad* is going to happen.

You see, in sales, you can either have a magic token that can change someone's life. Or you can be the threatening figure with a warrant to claim someone's possessions. The latter is *not* sales. Sales is the *former*. Sales, my friend, is about *giving* a gift you know you have—something that can *serve*.

Contrary to popular belief, selling (done properly) is <u>not</u> about taking something from someone else. Many people think that when they are selling they have to take something from someone else. Whether it's money, time—whatever they have to do they have to take—but that's not the way it needs to be. In fact, that mindset is what gets you in trouble. That mindset is what makes things hard. That mindset is what makes it not fun.

I was training some real estate professionals about a month ago—they were struggling. They were up to their eyeballs in marketing expenses—about $14,000 a month. And, after 4 months of investing in their existing marketing regime, they hadn't closed any deals. So, when I walked into the training room, everyone was ready to hear some revolutionary sales technique (from me). But, instead of sharing some far-fetched sales scheme, I just yelled out, "Stop selling houses! Stop selling real estate!"

The broker gave me a look, as to say "what are you saying?"". I paused for a few seconds, repeated myself, and then added, "...you need to focus on building relationships." As Tony Robbins said, *"You aren't in business to sell product or service. You are in the people business."* I taught this to the real estate brokers. And, that very same day, they put 3 houses in Escrow. AND, not even a month later, they put 12 houses in Escrow, and it has kept growing since.

The magic words that obviously sunk in were; **stop selling houses, start connecting with human beings**. That's what they did. They didn't have a sales problem. They didn't have a money problem. They had a *people problem*. They didn't understand how to *humanize* the whole experience. **You can't move product if you can't move people.**

The way I believe every business needs to look at it is that when we call someone or reach out to someone, **we approach them as if we are giving a gift.** I'm giving gifts every day. I'm handing out magic tokens. And so are you, whether you realize or not. When I wake up I'm thinking—who can I give my magic token to? Who can I help?

As many of my mentors have said, *if you want to make a million dollars, you have to give away at least a million dollars' worth of value.* Business is about helping people. If you want to earn more money, you have to *set aside* the money focus, and, instead, focus on how you are going to be of service to someone else's life. The more you help, the better you're going to do in business. So, what value will you bring to the world that's worth a million dollars? When you do that, and you focus on that value, success is inevitable. You're going to gain the revenue that you want (because you are being of **true service**).

The power of reciprocation is heavy. **People want to reciprocate.** They will pay you for the value that you give. If you are in business to *truly* impact lives for the better, you will succeed.

So, change your mindset. You have to first decide what you're going to give. And this comes back to what your business gives. Who is it, specifically, that you will help? This is something we will explore, in greater depth and dimension, in the coming chapters of the book. But remember, sales have nothing to do with taking. Selling *is about service; selling is about helping people solve their problems.*

I want you to think it through yourself. When you really need something, or when you're in pain, or things aren't going the way you really want—you buy stuff. You buy stuff that, hopefully, fixes your problems—your pain. If your car breaks down, every day for a month, would you still wait it out another month, or would you eventually get it fixed, perhaps even get a new car? Likely, you will get it fixed.

Now, if you're in pain, are you going to take painkillers? Or, are you going to try fixing it by finding a solution (that heals the root of your pain)?When something negatively affects your life, you are going to find someone who can help, or you are going to buy something that will help. **People love to buy things; especially when it takes away our pain or helps you with your desires.**

It comes back to being a great person, helping people gain their desires and get away from the pain. That's what business is built for. Why do people build businesses? To take away pain or to give new luxuries, right? That's pretty much almost everything—like any product or service—out there. They all add amenities to our life, to make things better.

Whether you are reaching people face to face, networking at events, promoting your business through social media, or making phone calls—I want you to imagine and step into the shoes of someone who is *always* there to be of service. Someone with an infinite supply of *magic tokens*, to give to people who you know, so each person you encounter (and provide with a token) walks away feeling better about his/her *value*. **Focus on the magic tokens you can provide**.

I'm assuming you want to be of true service to people's lives, truly, or you wouldn't be reading this book. I don't work with clients and businesses that don't care about people.

In my *Design It* course, I only focus on working with people who know they have a way to make a heart-felt impact on people's lives. I only work with those who truly want to add value to the lives of others. Over the course of three days, we take *action*, and put in *place* the systems needed to *transform* the destiny of their businesses. The results?—small tweaks, huge breakthroughs, and accelerated growth in their business revenues. And, more importantly, they get to bring that very special thing they have— their gift!—to market, and improve the quality of other people's lives. In exchange, their business and personal life thrives.

So, share your gift with the world, and you shall receive (the world!). All you have to do (to receive) is **be human, connect** with others humans, in a heartfelt way, and figure out exactly what they (each of your human clients) need, and how you can best serve them (and their needs).

But, what if they don't buy? What if they don't need or want what you have to give? You're probably thinking—"well then I lose out." Wrong. You don't lose. You both win. First, you don't spend your precious time and effort providing a solution they don't want. Second, you help them potentially move closer to a solution they do want and need. If you can't help them, then you refer them to someone or something else that can. If you can't refer them to someone else, or something else that can help, then tell them, "Hey, I would Google this. Go home and Google this, and I'm sure you will find something that will help you."

I always suggest pointing them in the right direction. But, no matter what, try to help every person you and your business interacts with. **They will remember you for that**. They will hold your business in high regard. You will build trust and brand equity in the market—people buy from businesses they trust (whether it's now, or later on down the road). The point is to be *consistent* in your intentions, and to be of *service* to someone.

CHAPTER 2

Setting Your Intention

"A good intention clothes itself with sudden power."
–Ralph Waldo Emerson

ntentions matter. Either you give the vibe of wanting to give, or you give the vibe of wanting to take. The latter promotes failure to sell and make an impact. The former opens *many doors* of opportunity—opportunities that allow you to deliver value, and get well paid for it. But, it begs a question, how is it that someone can guarantee they are presenting their truest most *positive* intentions for a customer? How can you demonstrate you actually care? It's a good question. First, I don't think anyone *doesn't* care. I think most people don't realize, or don't know exactly, *how* their care can be communicated to another human being.

For me, meditation has really helped me get grounded enough to feel confident in my every day interactions (including the way I communicate with others). I meditate every day (I'll talk more about this later). But, to start, I think you can do a *really* short meditation. One where you actually, before you make phone calls or before you go to a networking event, close your eyes for a few minutes and set an intention on what it is that you want and what it is you're willing to give. That intention changes everything. **When I imagine myself presenting a gift, a magic token that can improve someone's life, I'm looking forward to the call.** I'm in a space where I want to *understand*, rather than to *persuade*. I'm *listening* rather than doing too much *talking*.

Setting an intention is more important than any of the strategies that I have to teach you. This is why I'm beginning here (with teaching you the importance of intention).If you don't have the right intentions, you will cause struggle in your relationships, and, subsequently, your business.

So, just to show you how powerful intention can be, I'll guide you through a visualization. Please take a minute to find a comfortable seated position.

Now, close your eyes. Imagine the person you're going to help. If you know the person you're calling, picture his/her face, imagine looking into his/her eyes—what do you notice? Is it a picture? A word? Turn it up contrast and definition. Now, as you do, and as it becomes clearer, imagine projecting an intention to help and improve this person.

Without any thought to a product or service, just set the intention that you want to be **of service**. Notice the energy exchange that is occurring between the two now. As that energy reaches its peak, take a deep breath and come back to the present. Then, pick up your phone, send a message, or get on that teleconference call.

Remember: **you possess magic tokens**—gifts that you know *will* help this individual.

Notice it has *nothing* to do with a sales pitch. Instead of selling, you are setting the intention to be of service and help—you are curious to find out more about your client's life and business. It makes you want to ask questions (asking questions, **the right questions**, is something we will explore in greater detail in the coming chapters).

Setting an intention can turn any setback into a success. Here's an example: when I came out of film school, I built a production company that turned into a full ad agency. So I was looking for marketing directors—offering to take on all of their companies' marketing. I remember going in—they would always have me present previous campaigns and case studies. These were to promote ourselves and our capabilities in a way that we could possibly get new clients—which we would. But, as you remember, it was really hard to present that big pitch to 10+ companies *just* to get one. The presentation is usually not a small thing either. It was like a full song and dance; PowerPoint presentation, and pitching, pitching, pitching.

Side note: with what I'm teaching you now, you may never have to pitch again!

When I finally learned to *set an intention*, to understand how I could be of service, I no longer wanted to pitch. Instead, I was curious to understand. This shocked some people. I remember one marketing director's reaction in particular: when I walked in, he said, "Come on Steve, go ahead and plug in your laptop right here. Plug it into the big screen." I responded, "You know what, that won't be necessary right away." He said, with furrowed eyebrows (his "shocked face"):"What do you mean? You're not showing us anything? You don't have anything to show?"

They were talking like the meeting was almost over. But I said, "I'm not sure exactly what your needs are. What's going on presently, and what is your goal. Only then AND only then, can I actually know what to present to you. I don't want to be promoting oranges, if what you need is apples. Yes, they are both fruits. But they are different kind of fruits." The director pauses, thinks about it, and realizes that the logic marries up. So I take him through a line of questioning (which I'm going to teach you too), that empowered us to find out his companies' deepest desires, deepest pains, and deepest challenges—this process helped me discover his deepest needs, and address them.

So, remember, **intention is everything**.. Set that first. Then, ask the right questions, so that you can un-cover (and address) your clients' deepest needs. And, through this process, you have the ability to turn a potential customer into a *paying* customer. But, before that, I want to share in the next chapter, the *only two* things that can go wrong in any sales meeting, or any exchange. SO, here goes, onto the next lesson!

CHAPTER 3

Only TWO Things
Can Go Wrong

*"To effectively communicate, we must realize that we are all
different in the way we perceive the world and use this
understanding as a guide to our communication with others."*
—Tony Robbins

"What, are you crazy? Your hand is turning red. I can see
that your knuckles are turning white. You're slipping!
Grab my hand before you fall off the cliff!" That's
what I imagine myself telling my potential clients. I can't tell you
how many businesses I could have potentially worked with and it
was like they were hanging off a cliff, and I had the solution—I
was the helping hand that could save their businesses. I knew I
could help them. "Grab my hand. Grab my hand; I'm going to
help you. I'm going to save your business." Sadly, they respond
with something like, "No, thank you!"

"What, are you crazy?" I'm thinking. "You're going to fall off the cliff, take my hand now before it is too late!" They respond, "No thanks. No thanks. We're good. We're good." It blew my mind every time this happened, and I was just sitting there baffled. I'd let them play it out. Perhaps they saw something I didn't see, and things would work out for them. But surely enough, 6 months later, I would drive by their business and discover *there was no business*. They were out of business. Gone.

A part of me could be righteous and say, "Oh my goodness! I told you so!" But then, I realized, it was *equally* my fault—I was saying *the wrong thing*. You see, there are only two things that can go wrong when it comes to sales and marketing in your business. First, it's that you have a wrong potential client. So no matter how much you try to help them, they might not have wanted help anyway. And, even if they took you up on your solution, it would end up in disappointment because it was the *wrong match* for the problem they were having—selling a shovel to someone who wants the grass on their lawn to be cut.

Second, say you identify a valid client, like I did—the one that was hanging off the cliff. And you know you can help them. Then the *second* thing that could go wrong (and it did), is I was *saying the wrong thing*. That's it.

There are only two things that can go wrong:

1. The wrong match
2. The wrong message

That's it! There are only two things. **It's either the wrong person or the wrong message**. It's finding a semi-thirsty person and offering them water. They're not always going to accept that water. For example, if you tell them about how easy it is to pop the bottle cap, and how cool the bottle looks when you carry it in public—a thirsty person doesn't care. They want to know if it'll *quench* their thirst! But if you offer it in the exact right way that that person wants it, like "one sip of this and you'll forget what it's like to have a dry tongue", they're going to grab that water every time and drink it because they need it. They're thirsty.

So, every time you're growing your business, and you're not gaining the results you want, you have to look at those two things. Is it the right person? If it's no, then find a way to find the right person. If it's yes, and things don't work out, then we know you're saying the wrong thing to get them across the line.

How do you say the *right thing*? (We'll address it later in the book.) To say the right thing, you must use their words. That way, when you tell them what you have, they understand it and they resonate with it because you are using *their language* to create a connection (between you and your clients). And, because of this connection, they want to engage with you (and begin working together). It's about communication. I'm going to teach you how to find your perfect client, ask them what they want, and then communicate it in a way that they will get it. **It's that simple, three simple steps**. But, for now, I just want to share with you the *diagnostic* mindset you can use to identify the *problem* in your business, so you can focus on the *right solution*.

So, to sum it up: **get into the mindset** of doing everything you can to help. Then, **get curious**. Ask questions, try = to understand what your clients' deepest needs are. ,Then, from there, you can determine not only who your perfect client is, but also whether or not that person is the *right match* for what you want to provide. Once you have that right, the next step is *refining* what you should say to them so you can *both* win!

So in the next chapter, we are going to clarify your *perfect client*. Or what I call your **WOW client**. The client that makes your heart sing (and vice versa—you make their heart sing!). That way, everyone is excited and everyone has moved to the next level. This can be an effortless process—I'll show you how

You now have an opportunity to be greater than you've ever been before. But it won't be comfortable. I always say, success doesn't feel normal. What I mean by that is wherever you're going after a bigger goal, it is relatively unchartered waters. You might not know what it feels like where you're going. This is important to realize (and accept) because, when you step forward with the things that I teach you in this book, it won't feel normal. It's not going to be like what you have done before. **But give yourself permission to step forward**. Be a pioneer for your business, and a pioneer for your life. If you get nervous, or the butterflies— know it is normal. Accept it, **walk forward and remind yourself *why* you are doing what you do.**

It took me over a decade to figure these things out, and then another decade to refine them so that I could teach them, very easily and eloquently, to you. I've written *Capture Clients Close Deals* in such a way that it is easy for you to digest it, take action, using my proven strategies, and make change happen in your life and business. It might not happen overnight. But it will happen. And you most likely *won't* have to spend over a decade figuring it out!

PART TWO

Finding Your
Wow Client

CHAPTER 4

Only Work With
WOW Clients

*"Choose a job you love, and you will never
have to work a day in your life."*
—Confucius

He gave me 200,000 dollars and I fired him. Now before you start guessing why. I'm going to tell you. Basically, I felt overwhelmingly consumed in a negative way. There was a particular client I was serving, who really didn't want to be served, and didn't want to do business the right way. I won't go into details, but let's just say this client's way of doing business was *unethical.* As such, all my staff members were being drained and affected by it. Daily. Inspiration turned to desolation. In fact, I tried my best to turn it into a positive. But I couldn't deny the reality, this client was just *not* the perfect client I wanted. "Okay, I'm done." I told the client. "I can no longer work with you."

It was a tough decision, as this client was paying big dollars. And I brought an entire team in on the project, including one staff member who joined the team *just* for this project. Yes, my team was freaked out—this project helped pay the bills and their pay checks. But I had to tell them, "Listen, this was a bad client. It's not a good fit for us. It's destroying our morale and relationships with each other. From here on, we are going to divert energy to planning and acquiring *new clients* that we want to work with."

We did just that. Things ran smoother; we ended up securing *more* clients we liked, and making *much more money.* In other words, saying **goodbye** to the wrong client, lead to saying **hello** to a couple more clients that, in total, paid more, and made everyone on the team happy. As the New York Times bestselling author, and good friend of mine, John Assaraf says "Do more of what you love, less of what you don't, and *none* of what you hate." Same thing applies when you are working with clients. Choose the one that **wows** you. Do less of the ones that are okay, and **don't work** with the ones that you hate.

The trouble is, most business owners, entrepreneurs, and executives (that I meet) only have 1 or 2 **wow clients**. They have more OK or bad clients, what I call "Uh" clients, than WOW clients. More often than not, it's because these clients pay the bills, or because the business owners, entrepreneurs, etc. haven't asked them the right questions, beforehand, to really *qualify* their potential clients (before taking them on). Then, the majority of their clients and customers are just okay. Therefore, the business becomes a draining environment that serves draining clients.

It is these clients, when you get the phone call from them, you want to ignore the call. You do not want to take the call. Even worse than that, it is you waking up in the morning and knowing that you this "Uh" client that you have to meet—it ruins your whole day. You want to look forward to your day, not dread it—with draining clients, you are anticipating something negative rather than something fun. It actually becomes a cancer in your business.

"You want to know the difference between a dis-satisfied employee and a dis-satisfied business owner?" My friend Jon asks. I respond, "What's the difference?" Jon says, "The dis-satisfied employee complains about his boss. The dis-satisfied business owner complains about his clients." Jon couldn't have said it better.

So the solution is to work with your **wow** clients. People call these your perfect clients. But I refer to them as wow clients. **What I mean by a wow client is that your heart is beating faster every time you think of serving them.** You are super excited about the opportunity you've got to work with this client. And so are they. As a result of your interaction, you both get elevated to a higher energy level. As a result, it doesn't *feel* like work. It feels like inspiration, play, and an opportunity to make a serious difference. It makes your life happy.

It is actually better to focus on your wow clients. **You will actually get more clients because of how happy you are**. When you are happy, you radiate—you are magnetic. And, because you are positive and inspired, you will likely go the extra mile and do better work. This does wonders for your business reputation.

So, you can probably identify one or two clients that you would say are perfect. You just need to identify them for now. They are your wow clients. Our life is too short living with things that you do not want to live with. Make a decision to only work with the WOW—you have the power to choose who you work with and you do not work with. Many times businesses say, "Hey, I've got to take everything I can." Even on an executive level—maybe you are doing sales and bring in clients that you *think* you have to bring on—anything you can get because that is just the nature of business. This is not true.

You got into business to have autonomy. *Exercise it.* You *can* choose the work you do, **who you do it with, and the nature of the exchange for service.**

Right here, right now, I need you to *commit* **to working with more and more of your wow clients,** less of the okay ones, and *none* of your "Uh" ones. To do this, it's obviously not as simple as just dropping them immediately. More often than not, you have to plan your exit with these clients. And it's not going to happen overnight. You don't want to just fire them (unless they are that bad!) and have to go start your business over—not great for your cash flow. SO, two things you must do:

1. Don't take any more clients that are your nightmare clients. That's right. Say *no* to opportunities that lead to misery.

2. Start taking on only new clients that are wow clients.

3. Leave your "Uh" clients to someone else. Think about it, your "Uh" client could be someone else's wow client. That's right.

So you can find another provider for these "Uh" clients, and negotiate a *commission* for recommending them. The awesome thing is you can get paid. People will pay for these leads. Remember, it might not be perfect for you, but will be perfect for somebody else.

Case in point: I was working with a chiropractor. He did not like to work with the Workmen's Compensation clients. These are basically clients who have been injured on the job, and need chiropractic services. So, with any kind of Work Comp client or customer, he sent those patients to another chiropractor that actually really enjoyed the Workmen's Compensation clients. The chiropractor, that we referred them to, did not want to have as many patients, and he actually enjoyed his office time—filling out paperwork (there is a lot of paperwork for Workmen's Compensation clients).

So it is a perfect fit for them—whereas the other chiropractor (my client) did not like doing all the paperwork. He would rather do more sports medicine and help athletes overcome injuries—this takes more regular appointments—so it was the perfect trade-off. As a result, they started sending clients to each other, as a means of exchange. And the great thing about this is that when someone called my client's chiropractic office, with a Worker's Compensation claim, , my client referred them to the other office and they referred their athletic clients to him. And, another plus, he did not have to do the work. What if you actually got paid to refer a client you don't want to someone else? lHow cool is that?

So remember, there is always a way to prosper by saying no. You can hand off your non-wow clients, and get paid if you find a joint venture. You do not have to just throw the "Uh" clients away. You actually can get paid on these leads, and not have to do the work. How cool is that? I wish someone would have taught me this sooner in my business, because I too took on clients that I should have not taken on—I thought this was the way you made money. I thought you had to take everything you can get. Only taking on WOW clients would have saved me tons and tons of headaches, and tons of pain.

WOW clients—how do we find them? The next chapter tells you **exactly how to find your WOW clients**. The first thing to do is put a magnifying glass on the ones that we do have to see who out of our existing clients most *closely* matches your wow client.

CHAPTER 5

How To Find
Your Wow Client

"For me the greatest beauty always lies in the greatest clarity."
—Gotthold Ephraim Lessing

"I work with people who love and drive BMWs." That seems like an outrageous line. But let me explain. When you objectively want to find your Wow client, you have to observe how they live, and **identify the common threads** in their lives. In this case, if they all *drive BMWs*, wouldn't it be smart to either; go to BMW forums, buy a BMW, or subscribe to their email list or magazine? You know, for sure, that's where your client is. I had one real estate agent that completed my *Design It* course, and, as we did the exercise I'm about to share with you, he discovered that his *wow clients* all had swimming pools! Houses with swimming pools!

So guess what he did? He simply positioned and communicated himself as the *real estate agent* that helped people that wanted to buy or a sell a home with a swimming pool. And, as chances would have it, this real estate agent *also* had a swimming pool of his own. He was passionate about swimming pools.. So it was a perfect *wow client* match. Not only could he earn money by selling houses with pools, but he got to talk and share his *passion* about swimming pools. For other people, selling homes with pools might be a chore. For this particular client it was a *dream.*

So let's find that wow client for you. Let's get you in touch with them, because that will lead to a dream business and a dream life. For now, set aside your assumptions or what you *think* you know about your wow clients—doing this, setting aside assumptions, will allow you to **truly investigate** what the common threads really are (among your WOW clients). The answer may be surprising to you! It reveals itself as an unexpected moment that makes you go "Ah hah!" And all you have to do is follow the process I'm about to share with you in this chapter.

I would say about 6070% of my clients that go through this process, whether in my private coaching or in my *Design It* workshop, find that they are shocked at some of things that show up when they start really putting a magnifying glass on who their perfect client is.

Remember—only one of two things can go wrong. You either got the wrong client, or you are saying the wrong thing. So here is what I want you to do, right now—grab a pen and piece of paper. Or if you prefer to work on the computer, open a new blank document and get ready to type.

First, let's picture your wow client. The person you have *already* served and who makes your heart beat faster, who gives you a lift, and who you can't *wait* to serve. . Get out a piece of paper, a pen and a stopwatch (most of us can use our phones.) You can also **download the workbook accompaniment to this book at no charge here: <u>CaptureClientsCloseDeals.com/bonuses</u>**, and do this exercise there. Now imagine your favorite wow client. Who is it that comes to mind first? that—n

What if *none* of your clients have ever "wowed" you? Then imagine someone you would have loved to work with first, but have yet to work with. Or it may have been a client that you missed out on serving, but always thought, "Gosh I wish I could work with him/her!"

Typically, marketers call this a client avatar. But for us, we are calling him/her your wow client. Don't know who? Think about someone you have worked with before (client, colleague or the like), that you would love, absolutely adore working with. Not just because they pay, but because you love being around them, because you love interacting and collaborating with them. This exercise isn't about compromise. It is about really clarifying who your Wow client is or imagining that wow client (if you have not had one.) I want you to identify this individual.

Now set a timer for 3 minutes. Before you start the timer, let me tell you what I want you to do. During the 3 minutes, I want you to write as much as you can. This is for your eyes only, so if there are incomplete sentences, or misspellings, so what. The focus is on the content.

Here is what you are going to write about (as much as you can):

- What did this client gain from working with you physically? For example: If you are a chiropractor, maybe you helped a grandfather, with debilitating back pain, relieve his injury and the pain that goes with it. What was the physical service or product your client benefited from?

- What did they gain from this emotionally? For example: That same grandfather now can pick up his grandchild, increasing his connection with his family or maybe he no longer wakes up in the morning yelling at his wife, because he already started the day off in pain. What is the emotional gain your client received?

Start the 3-minute timer and write as much as you can about what the Wow client gained physically and emotionally. Go do it now.

Okay. You're back. (If you didn't do this exercise, put the book down and do it.)

This is important. When you understand how much of a difference saying *yes* to your service or product makes, you get the confidence and inspiration to really take it out to market and *help*! Remember, selling isn't about taking. Selling is about being of service!

Next, go ahead and draw a line under what you wrote or flip the paper over. The next part, of this exercise, is to use the same wow client and write for another 3-minutes. This time I want you to imagine the time you met the client (and were deciding whether or not to work with you). I want you to imagine that they said "NO." They chose NOT to work with you.

Now, write as much as you can in the 3 minutes about:

- What would your client have lost physically if they had not worked with you?

- What would have been emotionally lost?

Start the 3-minute timer. Write as much as you can about what the Wow client would have lost physically and emotionally. Go do it now.

Ok, are you done? Yes? Good.

Doing this helps you understand (and have confidence in) how *valuable* your service or business is to people's lives. This exercise is a very powerful thing—it shows you what people stand to lose (if they don't work with you). It really establishes what you are doing for other people, which is very powerful for your marketing purposes.

Okay. Now you're ready for the third part. Draw another line or flip the paper over. Set the timer for 5-minutes. Now start answering these questions (see below) as fast as you can.

- How old is this wow client?

- Do they have a family?

- Are they single?

- What kind of car do they drive?

- Where do they live?

- Where do they hang out?

- Are they on social media?

- What kind of social media, magazines or media do they subscribe to (e.g. Instagram, Facebook or LinkedIn)?

List anything that you can think about. Describe this individual and write down as much as you can. Even go beyond the physical attributes:

- What thoughts is this individual having?
- What emotions is this individual experiencing?

Maybe he or she wakes up in the morning with lots of energy, and looks most forward to spending time with family. I want you to get to the emotional triggers as well as the physical triggers. Just write everything you can down—do this as fast as you can. Don't worry about complete sentences, grammar, etc. I just want you to free write everything that you can think of. Forget about perfection. Just get it down.

Okay. You are ready. Start the timer and write as much as you can about this same Wow client (using as many of the above questions as you can.) Go.

This third part allows you to see a little deeper around who this person is, where they hang out, who they hang out with, and what social media they use, so you can find other people like them. And, guess what—people usually hang out with people very similar to themselves. So, if they are your wow client, chances are they hang out with more of your wow clients.

I'm so glad you used the last 11 or so minutes to write all this down. **These elements will help you so much.**

If you struggled answering some of these questions, the solution could be, and is most often the case, as simple as a phone call, or scheduling a phone call. Here's what you should say (when you call your WOW client): *"You are my perfect client. It is so amazing working you. If all of my clients were like you, I would be the happiest person alive. I'm curious; do you have a few minutes to answer some brief questions? This will help me better serve you, others like you, and make a greater difference in how I tend to my business.*

Most of the time they are going to say yes because they are so flattered that you are thinking of them as a wow client.

Once you have identified your WOW client, start hanging out with them. This is what I was talking about before regarding BMWs and swimming pools—start engaging in the activities that they like. Doing this—engaging in activities that your Wow clients enjoy—will help you establish what networking events are very important for you go to and which ones are not. It saves time in the long-run! Less effort for more results!

So, this process (that I just shared) is something you can do *multiple times*. In fact, I want you to repeat it. Once you have done it for one client you love, that one client you absolutely adore, you can repeat the process for a second (WOW client) and so on. You want to do this for about 6-12 wow clients minimum, so you can look at the results and identify the common threads. The patterns tend to emerge. You will start to see similarities between your wow clients, and the results might be *surprising*!

After you have 6-12 of these done, you can do the fourth and final part of the exercise. Lay the papers out on a table or hang them on a wall, get a highlighter, and mark all the commonalities.

Start to notice where all your wow clients overlap. This will give you clues about where you should spend your time, who you should spend your time with, and what you do for them.

You choose who you want to work with—clearly define who your WOW clients are. The clearer you are around this (who your WOW clients are), the more you'll attract in these types of dream individuals. Think about that real estate agent. You could say, "Hey, I work with people that want to buy or sell a house with a pool." Now, it narrows down your pool of potential clients. (Pun intended.) Not everybody wants a pool. Then there is the chiropractor I was talking about. He is no longer going to take on the patients with Work Comp. In fact, his favorites (clients) are sports injury. So he focused on that. "Hey, I work on people with sports injuries and they want to be rehabilitated through a chiropractic fashion versus surgery,"—by claiming this kind of work as his niche, he was able to gain attention from (and attract in) his perfect client.

Too often, business owners go about attracting clients in by using too general of approach—they say, "Hey, I work with everybody," or "Do you know anybody that is breathing? Anybody that is breathing, I can work with that!" Of course we know people that are breathing! But this way is so ambiguous that you tend to get absolutely no referrals—it is just too broad of a stroke.

But if you tell people something like, "Hey, I work with people who drive BMWs." Then they could say, "Oh, my friend, John, has a BMW. I could refer you to him," and it becomes very specific. Seem strange? It's not. Case in point: a car mechanic, who specializes in serving people who drive BMWs, might use this line.

Let me share a personal story with you. Remember my production company (that eventually turned into a full service ad agency)? When we were looking for marketing directors, I would just say, "We work with companies and we help them with their marketing." It was a struggle; we were not getting clients (no wonder!). This was in the 1990's, prior to social media really taking off. As a result of yet having access to the free to low cost marketing tools (offered by social media), it cost us a lot of money to do marketing.

We re-evaluated. We found that we were most successful with bigger companies—they needed to be generating a million or more in revenue. A million dollar business is technically still a small business, but, for me at that time, a million or more was a bigger client. These were also the sorts of projects we enjoyed more. So that was one of the first stipulations that I made. Even though there were still many types of companies, it was really beneficial for us to say "We work with companies that are generating a million or more in revenue, and we help them with their marketing." Not perfect, and still pretty broad, but that was the first step in beginning to establish some boundaries around who I was working with (and who I was not).

What happened next was amazing. I remember the first meeting I went—when I finally decided to communicate this. At first, all the people in the room were people I figured weren't earning at least a million dollars. They were much smaller businesses, but I still decided to declare my statement anyway, *"We typically work with businesses that are making a million or more."* After I said that, someone approached me and said, "Hey, I have a friend—his business is up to 1.2 million, and they had a plateau. I am sure he would love to talk to you." I got the lead from the very people that I thought were not even going to be able to help me. All I had to do was communicate my *wow client* message.

I cannot stress this enough: **define your WOW client!** When you do this, you declare it out loud, to the world, that this is your perfect client. AND, you shall receive—you WILL attract more of these perfect clients, these WOW clients. Science has shown this. There is a part of our minds called the Reticular Activation System (RAS)—it sorts and filters information from your environment, based on what you focus your mind and heart on. Here's an example:

There you are sitting—reading this book—as you start to focus on seeing the color blue, close your eyes and think about it. Now open your eyes—how much of the color blue do you notice? A lot more blue, right? The same thing happens when you focus, define, and think about your wow client.

The more you have them on your mind, the more they show up in your life. This is exactly why we want to identify who they are, and then dig deep through the exercises (that I shared in this chapter). Figure out who they are, what they are doing and where are they, then declare, out loud (to the world), that this is the kind of client you want to work with. If you need help crafting your message—to attract in your dream clients—stay tuned—I will teach you that in the coming chapters.

When you go and you call these wow clients and you are figuring out what the best approach is, you are going to be able to ask the right questions. This is also going to help – remember I was talking about finding your perfect client. Ask them what they want that is also what we want. We are going to take it beyond finding out about them.

Now that you know who your wow client is, we are going to dig deeper (in the next chapter) and find out more about what it is they want, and how you can best serve them. That way, it is a win-win. By getting clear around your dream clients' pain and desires (both things that motivate them)—you can connect with them on a deeper level. You can communicate precisely, using their words, to gain their trust, to build rapport, and to *close the deal*. I will teach you exactly what to say to *capture clients,* and to *close deals.*

It's simple. **Define and declare** your wow client. **Make sure the messaging is right**—remember: these are the only two things that can go wrong. But, when you get it right, you are in for some **huge** success in your business; more fun, more revenue, more freedom.

PART THREE

Stop Guessing And
Start Knowing
What Clients Want

CHAPTER 6

It's Simple…
Ask Them!

*"I don't guess. I think. I ponder. I deduce.
Then I decide. But I never guess."*
—William Goldman

"What's the greatest value that your patients receive from working with you? My customers want pain relief! I know they want pain relief!" That's what my client said. I could see the passion coming from him. I could tell he wanted to share more. So I let him continue. "I had a grandfather that had so much back pain that he couldn't even pick up his grandchildren. After my treatment, he was able to pick up his grandchildren—what a huge emotional connection. Anyone who has children, and grandchildren, know how precious it is to hold them. This was life changing. It was more than just helping people with their back pain. I was changing their life."

I responded, "Wow! That's amazing. I'm so glad you know exactly what *impact* you have on your client's lives! It's exactly what we want—to impact the the most amount of clients possible (with your service).." This chiropractor was doing all right in his business. But he wanted more business, so he brought me in. Now, if he was so certain that pain relief was his customers' primary want, and he knew who he wanted to serve, then I knew that one of two things had gone wrong—his messaging was either off, or he had the wrong client. But by the sound of it, the *wow client* was right on. He was passionate, inspired about talking about that client, and certain in the value he delivered. So my suspicion—he had the wrong messaging

He was guessing. And my simple solution to finding out what the *wow client* wants; **ask**. It's that simple. We find our *wow* client, and we just asked them what they want! I wish someone had told me this 10 years ago.

Is "asking" really just a survey, Steve? (You may be wondering this.) Yes and no. People call it surveying. I call it **asking**.

Here's why: people are sick and tired of surveys.. Sure, surveys work. But the way to get real quality results from the clients—show them some appreciation, show them you care, then ask for some data. It's more about asking the right questions, and treating people like people. It's a mindset thing. I want to drill home that no matter how good your systems or tools are, it's about people. **If you can't move people, you can't move products/services.**

Back to the story: So I said to my client "Now, can I talk to your *wow* patients about this? Just to confirm?" and I told him the importance of finding out what the patients want. And he said,

"Sure." So we asked the patients and compiled their responses. You'll never guess what came back. It was on-time appointments. That's right, before pain relief, they wanted on-time appointments. That was their most frustrating experience, and on-time appointments were the solution. Sure, people said pain relief as well. But by far, (about 60% more) of his wow clients were saying *on-time appointments*. It was the *single* largest piece of feedback.

With this in mind, I went to the doctor and I said "Hey, on-time appointments are the most frequent response that came back." He responded, "I'm shocked! But then I'm not shocked in the same sense …" he continued "I do not like waiting at a doctor's office. Before being treated for my illness, my first point of pain is actually *waiting* while being in pain." It made sense. How many of us have sat in a waiting room, for 15, 30, if not 60 minutes, just to get attended to? It's frustrating. If this has happened to you, you know exactly what I'm talking about.

The client (chiropractor) told me he completely disliked it. So I said, "Well. How on time are you? How many appointments do you typically make it on time for?" He responded honestly and said "About 60 to 70 percent." We then looked at the stats and compared it to other doctor's offices—his ratings were pretty high. This probably explained why a lot of clients liked his service.

But I didn't go straight to the solution yet. I asked another question. "What if you were 90, 95, or even 100 percent on-time to your appointments?" And he said, "Hey well the patients would have to be in on it. It would be a no brainer for them!" So the first action we took was to get his receptionist to take calls and ask every customer that was making an appointment (say for illustrative sakes, Tuesday 9:30 AM), "How would you like to see the doctor right at 9:30 AM?" The patient responded, "Of course! Yes. It would be great to see him at 9:30 on the dot." The receptionist then responded professionally, and said "Okay great. We just need one thing from you. We need you to be on time. If you are 5 minutes or more late, we have to cancel the appointment." They agreed (of course). They showed up. Then we said, "If you know you are going to be late, call ahead of time and we will reschedule you as soon as we can. We can't promise the same day, but we'll do our best."

They agreed to the terms. It was all about good communication. This was the protocol I helped him develop. I got the receptionist to continue with this protocol, and, within a month, we already noticed an *increase* in his business. People started talking about their clinic, telling their friends and family, etc.

Every time that the receptionist answered the phone, she said, "home of the on-time appointment," everything was about the on-time appointment, and we learned this by *asking* for feedback from his clients and patients—this was the only tweak we made.

Then we put billboards out in his area. The billboard did not read *pain relief*, it read *on-time appointments*. We tweaked just *two* words! Then we added, "When your on-time the doctor is on-time." We received SO much positive feedback (and business) because of this simple strategy—new patients would tell us that they found out about the chiropractic clinic via the billboard. We had people say, "We were driving back to work late from our other chiropractor, and so we decided to switch chiropractors. We needed on-time appointments."

This particular chiropractor went on to grow 10 clinics. You can guess what that meant for his revenues. He was able to sell his clinics, and retire—owning property around the world. He's done very, very, well. He's not even 50 years old! The catalyst—getting the right messaging—he moved from rom *pain relief* to *on-time appointments*. From there, we designed his business to support the marketing message for his wow clients. He differentiated himself from other chiropractors talking about pain relief.

I've completed this process with many of my clients—about 70 percent are shocked with the information that comes back when they simply *ask* their wow clients, what is most important to them. They have an "Ah hah!" moment because they hear something they hadn't heard before. And only about 30 percent get the validation they are saying the right thing. Which is fine, because they are getting confirmation that they're doing the right thing.

A similar thing occurred with another company. When I worked with them, they were talking about high customer service, quality reports and that was the promise written all over their website. When we did the survey, the most common response was *quick turnaround* time. Not surprisingly, there was one sales person who was outperforming the rest of the sales people. When we presented the results of the survey to him, he said, "Oh my gosh, that's all I sell! Just quick turnaround time. What do the rest of the sales people sell?" Obviously not that.

So what did we do? We changed the content on their website to quick turnaround times. Just after that, they started getting call-ins off the website, and one of their receptionists had to tend to inbound calls, and learn how to process sales! The receptionist who had no training in sales, yet she was closing deals. Meanwhile, they had salespeople having trouble making sales because of the wrong verbiage. **Remember what I said? Either you have the wrong customer or the *wrong message.***

Case in point: you don't have to chase nor do you have to convince. **If you say the right thing to the right people, you can gain clients simply because that is what they <u>truly want.</u>**

So remember what I was saying... find your **perfect client, ask them** what they want and **then give it to them.** So if you ask them, and they want the color red, then you tell them "We have the color red, right here waiting for you." That's all. We don't say burgundy or make it any different. **We don't make up some other shade of red because we think it sounds cool.**

We actually say the exact words. This is called **back-tracking**. I'll share more on that later in this book as we explore more *advanced* and *amazing* strategies.

Another case in point: I had a financial company in San Francisco. When we asked their wow clients, we found out that their clients most valued the *free parking*. This particular financial company had a parking lot and it was free to clients and guests. If you know San Francisco, parking can be very difficult and quite costly. So guess what we want to communicate to get clients to show up at the office (or to get them to *consider* even coming in for a consultation)?? You got it! We told them *free parking.*

Before we tie up this chapter, I need to remind you of something important. If your message is great, and matches your perfect wow client, you *still* have to be able to deliver on your service. If not, you have a bigger headache. For example, does that chiropractor I told you about still have to make sure his businesses provide the pain relief? Absolutely! We still want to have that great service. We still want to have good financial advice even if we get free parking.

Client acquisition is important, but client retention is equally as important. If you can't deliver on your promise, *don't* be in business—simple as that. I'm simply teaching you how to make sure the people you want to serve, *get served*. I just presuppose you haven't got a fulfillment problem. You just have one of two potential problems; you've got the wrong client, or you have the wrong messaging.

It's the smallest things that attract our clients. It might be something completely different, completely out of your capacity to guess. And guess what? You don't have to guess anymore. You can go ask them. Just ask them, ask them, ask them etc.

You see, it's really easy to fail in advertising especially if you get too creative. That's what I did. I came out of film school and started creating ads and I failed. I got so creative and created movie-like ads that I thought were going to be a hit and they failed. And they failed because I failed to ask what the client wanted. I failed to discover what was the most important for those clients. The less creative you are and the more you pay attention to what your clients want, you're going to win because now you're not guessing. So take the creative part out, ask the clients what they want, put it in your ads, put it in your message, put it in when you're talking to them. You do that, and you're going to win.

CHAPTER 7

Survey To Success

"The art and science of asking questions
is the source of all knowledge."
—Thomas Berger

"You read my mind! How ...?" I didn't. I just asked a question. In this chapter, I share about how we can go about surveying our clients, to get the data we need in order to deliver the right messaging. So the first rule in surveys is what I mentioned earlier in this book—**do not call it a survey.** *Do not* call it a survey unless you can really come across as being of help or service.

You want to relate to it as a helpful call where you want to understand, and express gratitude for your wow client. You can do this with a simple call and question, "Hey, I want to help you the best that I can. Do you have three minutes to answer three questions?" And if it's a potential client, usually I only ask two questions (I'll share them with soon). But the first thing I'll say to a past client, who is a model for my wow client, is "It only takes three minutes to answer three questions so I can better help you and others like you in the future."

Most of the time, people are going to say yes—because you are approaching with the intention to understand and help out You aren't trying to sell them. You want to be of service. This is what we covered in the first section of this book. Service, service, service! If you come in with that approach, why wouldn't the person on the other end of the line want you to be better at what you're doing? Of course they would. Then you say, with transparency and authenticity, "I want to help–I want to take my business to the next level. I want to help people more than I ever have before, and, in order to do this, I need to have some quality feedback from you. You are one of those customers that I'd love to work with more. If I could work with more people just like you, I'd be overjoyed. So I'm not going to take a lot of your time. I just want to take three minutes and have you answer three questions. Would you be willing to do that for me so I can better serve you?"

You are going to get a yes. Unless you really got them at a bad time, people are going do it. Or, the worst case, they will reschedule with you. It's all about your intentions.

Next thing: remember that even if they said yes, you have to respect their time. Keep it as simple and short as possible. People don't have time to answer a lot of questions. They have busy lives just like most people who are making a living do. For people who have clients they regularly speak too, you can just bolt on the three minutes' worth of questions towards the end of your call. For example, say something like "Hey, real quick before we get off. Can I just ask one quick question?"

Then what you can do, in your database or in your contact/address book or notepad, you can write in what their answer was. Then the next time you're on the phone with that client, you can ask the next question and you can have a whole list of questions and just keep asking questions, getting more feedback, and finding out more information. In no time, you will have the information you need so you can better serve more of those customers in the future.

The next thing you need to know; **you need to have open-ended questions**. You do not want to ask, "Hey how is your pain relief on a scale of 1 to 10?" Yes, you're going to get a little bit of information of how good of a job you've done and that can be worthwhile, but in this case, it does not serve you. It does not help you find out what the *key message* is that you need to communicate it.

Think about it, if we had done that with the chiropractor I shared about, we would have never known that on-time appointments were going to get their attention and get them excited. So a sample open-ended question would be, "What is the greatest value that you gained from working with me?" That's one of my favorite questions. Take note of this question. Ask the question, and then all you need to do is *listen* attentively, take notes and give them space to respond and organize their thoughts.

I'm telling you right now, you want their words. You need their words because what they say is what you're going to put in your advertising. As David Ogilvy (advertising legend) said, *"I don't know the rules of grammar. If you're trying to persuade people to do something, or buy something, it seems to me you should use their language."*

How else can you solicit information rich answers? Another thing you could ask is—"What would be one thing that we could add or improve to make the experience better?" Let them answer. Or you could ask, "what, specifically, is one thing that attracted you to our service?" You could also ask, "What's the biggest thing you've gotten from our service?"

Now, notice that these questions are all about *the greatest value, the biggest thing,* the *one thing,* etc. They're all singular. BUT, they are also open-ended—this allows for the question to be answered quickly (as we promised them when we called). If you just say, "Hey, what did we do well?", you might get a long-winded (and all over the place) response. **You want to get information on what's the biggest, what's the most important thing, and what's the number one thing.** Those are the type of questions you want to ask.

Now, those questions are useful for clients you have served. **But if you are talking to potential clients, you want to ask two specific questions.** First, you want , to express what your biggest goal or desire is right now. So if I get on the phone with a potential client, I would express how excited I am about my business and maybe share one of my goals that I have and then say, "Goals are a really big thing for me, I'm really curious about your goals. What is one of your biggest goals right now?" Then let them tell you the goal. And then I repeat the goal back to them and make sure that I heard it right. I then ask "And let me ask you, what is slowing you down or stopping you from achieving this goal?" Now I've also got their biggest challenge. The beauty of this is that they're telling you what their biggest goal and what is their biggest challenge is. If you can help them with that, it's beautiful.

People often think that surveying clients after they receive the product or service is important. It is. After all, the majority of businesses don't survey at all. They don't even ask their clients for feedback. However, that's not such an issue. The most important time to survey your clients is at the beginning, when they are potential clients—when you meet them before they formally become a client.

Think about it, if you ask them what they want, before you work with them, wouldn't that be a better time to find out what they want, rather than at the exit when you're done with the project? If you only ask them at the end, all you will realize is, "You know, it would have been really nice if you would have done this or you would have done that, etc." Too late—it is already done. Yes, maybe that will help you for the next time, which is great.

When clients come and meet with me, in a private consultation, we start with a strategy session to go over their business. For my private clients, I ask them "Hey, we are going to look at where you are in your business, where you want to go, and then we're going to see how we can get you there faster. Maybe we'll be able to work together, maybe we won't, but at least it will give you clarity in the direction you're going to go." Similar thing stands for participants in my *Design It* course (in a group setting).

After they answer my question regarding their goals, I ask, "Before we get started … what would have to happen right now, in this meeting, for you to leave and have more excitement than you thought you would have?" And guess what happens when you ask them this question? They tell you. They tell you what they want.

The secret to getting more clients is asking lots of quality questions. I'm asking a lot of questions to find out what's going on. And it's just like what I'm talking about for surveying right now. It takes all the guessing out.

I was just teaching my *Design It* workshop this past weekend, and we were talking about **a lead magnet**—a tool that business owners use to grab client's attention and to see if potential clients are a right fit (for the business). A lead magnet also allows a business owner to capture a potential client's contact details so the business relationship can be built. So we do what we normally do, we ask the question "What is something good that you can give away?" A lot of the times, a lead magnet is something that you give away to all your potential clients—a gift, right? It's not something you charge for, it's something that you give away for free, and it's valuable enough that the person would have happily paid for it. So one business owner got up and asked "Hey, what is going to be valuable for my clients?" **And I smiled and said, "Why don't you ask them?** Ask your potential wow clients, what's going to be the most valuable for them? Then give them that."

Just think how simple this is, unbelievably simple. It takes all the guesswork out of it. It makes business so simple. If you've been working on the previous chapter's exercise and you've done it a few more times to really define who your wow client is, then guess what the next step is, go, ask that perfect client what they want. Go ask them questions, ask them if they have a few minutes to answer some questions so that you can best serve them. Ask them the questions, write down exactly what they say or, even better yet, record it (with their permission). Alternatively, if you need a survey tool, use *SurveyMonkey*. With *SurveyMonkey* you can start out free (up to 100 surveys), and then, if you want to pay for the next level, I think it's like 10 or 20 bucks. Either way, it's really cheap, especially since you are going to gain *quality* information about your clients.

As you know, I've literally taken words from surveys and put it into my clients' ads—. And of course, they start gaining more clients. In comparison, if somebody was blasting us with advertisements and it wasn't what we wanted, we would tune it out.

So I can't stress it enough, survey all the time—survey at the beginning, survey at the end, survey during. You are doing it to *gain* market intelligence.

So, a quick synopsis of what we have covered in this chapter:

One: Don't call it a survey. **Two:** Keep it simple and short. **Three:** Use open-ended questions. **Four:** Keep it singular **Five:** "Survey" all of your potential clients (before they're a client). Ask them **a.** what their biggest goal is **b.** what their biggest challenge is, so you know if you can help them or not

If you do these five things, it's going to be really simple for you to craft the right message.

It's so powerful. I will tell you, out of all the advertisers and marketers that I have been with (and I've been with some very high-end masterminds and some of the top marketers in the world)—we all have agreed—the campaigns that win were all the ones where we had surveyed ahead of time. We found out what the customer wanted, and then we delivered our campaign based around that.

Now, if you are running marketing, and you're spending money on marketing, and not getting the results you want, then one of the big things you can do, right now, is stop the marketing. Stop the marketing for a whole month, take that entire budget and apply it towards gifts for anybody that fills out your survey. If you don't know, for sure, what your clients value, want and need, it's all guess work—SO; survey, survey, survey.

I had one client that is in the apparel industry—working with Olympians. The company actually featured (and sold) hats signed by Olympic athletes. They gave those hats away if people completed their survey. They put it into a drawing, and they pulled names out a hat. For everyone else who didn't win the draw, they got to purchase other merchandise in their online store at a 15 percent discount. Other clients of mine have given away a $5 Starbucks card, and they say, "Hey, take three minutes and answer three questions and I'll buy you a cup of coffee." It can be that simple.

It could also be an Amazon gift card, but it is going to cost you a bit more money. The good thing is you're going to gain the information you want—which is super valuable. It could be worth hundreds of thousands of dollars if you start communicating properly to your perfect client. It gives you a huge leg up. It's worth every penny that you're going to spend.

Think about it, even if you're not spending money on marketing, but you're going out to networking events, isn't it important to know what your clients want so you can talk about that? Wouldn't it be worth even paying for that information, so that you know, over and over again, what to say? It's going to pay for every penny of what you gave away.

Give you another example. Our *Design It* course is a $2,000 course. Well, it actually costs $1,997.. We promote online, and via more and more podcasts and radios shows. We have people from all parts of the world attend; Australia, Singapore, Canada and all around the United States. I don't want to travel the world teaching all the time, of course. Some of my speaker friends do—but I want to be able to be with my children. Problem is a lot of my clients from overseas have the struggle of investing in an overseas flight ticket to get to the event.

Knowing this, I created a $1,200 travel voucher, this year. What we do is we discount the ticket price and we take that $1,200 off, so then attendees only have to invest $797 to come to the course. They apply the $1,200 toward their air fare, transportation and/or accommodations. But, in order to get this travel voucher, guess what you have to do? They fill out a survey. I don't call it a survey. I say it's an application where they get the travel voucher. It's is $1,200 off—they are going to fill it out! And, as a result of this exchange, I'm able to get more information about my customers, so I can better help them.

Remember, you are in the business of making a difference in people's lives—a contribution. That's something you have to keep in mind every time you interact with your clients. I'm giving them $1,200 discount off the course and that's a huge incentive for them to come. And I'm also being transparent with you—that allows me to stay home. So, if people are willing to come to me, I give them a discount. I make less money, but guess what? I get to stay with my kids *and* I get to demonstrate that I care enough about my wow clients—that I want to help them get what they want in life and business. Before we finish this chapter, this is something I want to drive home.

By demonstrating upfront value, you are proving yourself to your customer. You are gaining their trust, and their good will. This can't be underestimated. In the next chapter, I will teach you how to use your perfect client avatar, and your survey, to formulate the exact message that's going to attract more clients to say yes.

You will learn how to craft the perfect message in 30 seconds (60 seconds max)—this is empowering! And there's no guess work (in creating your message)! **The puzzle pieces are lining up—it's going to be a beautiful thing.**

PART FOUR

The Right Message

CHAPTER 8

Your Audio Logo

"In the modern world of business, it is useless to be a creative, original thinker unless you can also sell what you create."
—David Ogilvy

H e chose to die in his car. That's what one gentleman did. He was faced with a life-threatening situation, which could be treated, but there was a catch. He was nearly 100 miles away from the medical facility. He told his wife to drive him to the hospital instead of getting air lifted out. He was worried about the medical bills his family would have to deal with. He didn't have that sort of money. "Honey, I don't want that sort of burden on us and the family." That's what he told his wife. And that's similar to what other widows shared, after my team interviewed them. Where am I going with this? Aside from being heart-wrenching and sad beyond measure—this is an example of how *life-saving* understanding your wow clients can be (and how profitable it can be for businesses who serve their customers *greatest* needs).

My *air medical transportation* client learned how *life-saving* understanding his clients could be. When I worked with them they were saying all different kinds of things about the value of their service, including; how effective their airplanes were, how safe their helicopters were, fast-response times etc. Put simply, they were fast, responsive, and safe. But their business—they created a gap Insurance policy which was called a membership. As part of that membership they covered your *out-of-pocket*. But, as you probably already know, there's lots that is not covered as part of medical insurance. So it could be $7,000 to $20,000 out-of-pocket that's not covered. That's what we discovered when we surveyed people. There were people who chose *not* to be flown for medical treatment, and died in their car! People lost their loved ones because they didn't want the financial burden.

As soon as this company saw this, they created a new membership program that addressed this issue. The problem—it was a costly and riskier thing to run. So in return, they had to make sure they *acquired more customers* for *less*. It was costing them over $120 to acquire a new member and their membership only earned them $50 a year. So that means it would take 3 years for them to make their money back and that doesn't even count any flight cost. That just didn't work.

So, through the survey, we figured out the right words. The ad that we came up with was: "*My life was saved and my bill was covered for fifty dollars.*" Simple. And it worked! This program went from almost closing their membership program to actually flourishing—having over a million members and 65 million in revenue a year. It came back to their message.

Up to this point, we've talked about who your perfect client is and what they want. We survey to ask them what they want, so we can give it to them if we have it. **Now, let's talk about giving them the right words.** *How you say it will be as important as what you say.* That's why we survey. Let's say we go on a journey together—we go on a hike one day. If, at the end of that hike, we were to write a journal of what happened (on the hike) my journal is going to be different than yours. One: because we see things differently. Two: because it's likely we are going to *say* things differently—even if we have common experiences. It's the same thing with clients. They're all going to see things in a different way, and every person is going to use different words. After you survey them, you take the average response. As mentioned before, you find the common pattern. It's not going to be 100% spot on. But it'll be close enough. **It'll be better than guessing.**

To get to a simple message that works, or what I call an *audio logo,* involves surveying and understanding your clients. You must understand who they are, the pain they are experiencing, and the gain they stand to get. Back to my *air medical transportation* client: We started surveying in rural Texas—rural areas are directly affected by air medical transport—to be flown, you need to be in rural areas. If you are in a major metropolitan area, you don't need to be flown (in most cases). So when people clicked on the *"My life was saved and my bill was covered for fifty dollars,"* they arrived on a web page that said, "Hey! You live in rural Texas?"

Now, one thing to note: when you answer the question "who it is for", it's sometimes obviously implied in the ad. It's not always directly stated, such as "I work with executives of million dollar companies." That's something to bear in mind. As a side example, I had another client that worked with eating disorders and helping people lose weight—and she worked with extreme cases , such as bulimia to anorexia. The words we came up with from the survey were, *"Imagine how your life might be different if you didn't have to watch your eating or your weight."* People with bulimia or anorexia watch their weight all the time! So the audience is implied (as opposed to directly stated) .

Back to the air medical transportation business. After we identified that we were working with people from rural Texas, we connected with their pain. "We know it's an unbelievably terrible thing to have an accident that worsens your financial situation afterwards, bills stacking up etc." That's a huge pain. Then, after that, we said, "For as little as $50 we're going to cover your out-of-pocket expenses." That's a *huge* gain! In this particular example, of the air medical transportation company, the pain was "saving a life and the enormous medical bills that go with being flown." and the gain is "it's covered for only 50 dollars."

Now, the next two components are about *communicating* to their pain and to their gain. I will cover these two simultaneously. First, because *pain* is what motivates people to take action, most people look to *avoid* or *get away* from pain. Those customers are *ready* to take action because they have a pressing problem. How many times have you bought something out of urgency for pain relief? You wanted to get out of that pain. Or imagine that your shower only ran cold water, every day, for a month! You are likely to figure out a way to get a new shower head or repair it … right? Or if you're in physical pain, like back pain, you're going to try anything to get relief! Now, the pain doesn't have to be physical. It just has to have enough charge that the person will want to take action.

But isn't talking to their pain manipulative? Isn't that getting someone into a state of being negative about life? That's what some people often think. But you're not. Your message is simply bringing their focus to a pain that is already there. And, by doing that, you are creating the potential for them to take action for a solution. This leads me to the next point. Second, because *gain* is coupled with *pain*, it is what gets people to take *serious action*. Just like in an electronic circuit—the reason electricity flows is because there is a *positive* and a *negative*. Or, imagine this—you are walking in a desert and you are thirsty and uncomfortable. You are searching for water everywhere—dragging your feet, hoping and praying that you will find an oasis. Then, suddenly, from a distance, you can see an oasis. It comes into view. As *soon* as it comes into view, you will start to run right towards it. Why? Because both *pain* and *gain* are evident! **That's what causes *action*.**

Let's take a look at *Star Wars: Episode IV A New Hope* Remember when they were on the Death Star and they had to save Princess Leia? So there they were, Luke Skywalker, Han Solo, and Chewbacca. They battle the Stormtroopers and they bust the princess out of her jail cell. Celebration! But then, as they are escaping, they get trapped in a garbage bin with walls that are about to compact them alive. And, in that bin, is a serpent that attempts to drag Luke underwater and kill him. Bad news! Gladly, the robot (R2D2) stopped the compactor, and they busted out of the place just in time. Phew! Relief. Resolution.

This up-down-up-down thing is characteristic for anything that engages. It's called life. It's those kind of movies that grab people's attention, keep them hooked, enthralled and surprised, before they get resolution.

So remember, you have to survey them. Then you create the message that communicates; who it is for, their pain, and their gain. Here's another example. I was working with a mortgage broker who used to say, "*Hey, I help people buy homes or refinance their home.*"—this isn't bad. But we could do better. After surveying her client, we decided to change the message to, "*Typically, I work with people who are curious about home finance options, who may be confused with the overwhelming information and programs out there, and are afraid that making the wrong decision could cost them dearly.*"

So we connected with who the audience was, and their pain. Then she went on to say, "*I help my clients find the right loan and the right program, which has saved my clients tens of thousands of dollars, and, in some cases, six figures, over $100,000.*" She communicated what the gain was!

For my audio logo (I have three), but here's the general gist (what I say): "*Typically, I work with entrepreneurs/C level executives/ Coaches/Consultants who are struggling to grow their business as fast as they'd like and/or even if they have the money coming in, they are working way too hard. They are tired of trying to figure it out on their own and don't know who to turn to for the right advice. As a direct result of working with me, my clients make millions more in revenue, and gain more time and energy to enjoy their personal life.*"

These words came right out of the surveys. I simply organized it into; who it is for, what they are struggling with, and what they most want—to *regain* their life. Now in comparison, notice how dull these following phrases sound:

- "I'm an accountant."

- "I'm a chiropractor."

- "I'm a consultant."

- "I'm a lawyer."

They should. All three are examples of answers most people give to the question, "What do you do?" And they are also answers that mean *doom* to your business. Yes, they are appropriate in some contexts in terms of positioning. But in terms of *communicating* what you do to your wow client—they fail.

Let's go back to the cliff-hanging example. Remember how I sometimes feel like I am telling clients *"Grab my hand!"* And they're like, *"No thanks, I'm fine."*? Well, clearly they needed my help. So I realized, it wasn't the *wrong* client—it was my messaging.

So we ask the person hanging off the cliff, "Is there something I can help you with?" Then they might say, "Well yeah, I'd like to have a rope—if I could have a rope that'd be great." Then I would go grab a rope, and dangle it in front of them, in my hand. So they would grab the rope *and* my hand. Then I'd be able to pull them up! Sure, it happened to be that that individual was set on having the solution of the rope (when a hand would suffice). But changing their focus takes a lot more work. It can happen, absolutely. But it's not as efficient. The most efficient way is to use the right words. *Their words.*

I can't stress it enough—**who's it for, what's their pain and what is the gain.** Putting it into this format, gives you all the power. By utilizing their words, you can help them get up from the cliff.

In the next chapter, we are going to talk about how we start to ask the right questions. This is something we mentioned earlier in the book. But we are going to peel the layers back. There are always more layers. The more fine-tuned we get, the better you get at *capturing more clients* and *closing more deals.* So, we will cover what questions you need to ask, and more ways you can use the right questions to get the information you need. Going deeper (with my questioning) has allowed me to go from being a 1 out of 10 salespersons, which I thought was effective, to a near 2 out of 3. In fact, a lot of the times it is 100% conversion. If it's the right client, and I get them in front of me and I use the right language, they're going to work with me, because it is the right fit. The 1 out of 3 that I don't end up working with me is because I choose not to take them on. **I choose**. Not them. And I want that for you. You want that for you, don't you? That's right. So let's move on.

PART FIVE

More People Buy To Get Rid Of Pain

CHAPTER 9

RAPPORT

"Trust is the glue of life. It's the most essential ingredient in effective communication. It's the foundational principle that holds all relationships."
—Stephen Covey

Your clients don't trust you. You are a threat to their safety. And, like any person who is in flight or fight mode, they are awake and aware and waiting for you to pounce. When you meet someone new or you get into a sales engagement, that meter (fight or flight) is likely up on high because it's a stranger, so you are still unconsciously or consciously asking, "Is this person safe? It goes back to that basic thing, "Is there a lion or a tiger that's going to jump out and get me? I *need* to know…." But you don't know them yet. You are guarded—that's not saying that you are a bad person or anything (it just means you are "feeling' out a new situation).

And, even worse, when you're in a sales thing where a potential client might buy something, he/she is even more guarded—that real estate broker (your potential client) might be thinking: "Okay, this person is going to pause and try to take something from me. Are they operating with integrity?" If you don't pay attention to the person in front of you, it could end un-favorably—with you not *closing the deal*.

There's not much space to serve someone if they won't let you into their world. In business—this means there is a *barrier* to exchange. So why do I mention this? Because you need to know this *before* you try to sell and serve someone. Until you get to the depth of what they are experiencing, in terms of pain and what they most want, it will be a hit and miss in terms of you serving them in a much larger way. They won't answer your questions truthfully. Remember, we want to communicate a message that connects with them—that shows we can ease their pain (or even "cure" it) and help them realize (and achieve) their deepest desires.

Find out who they are, find out what their pain is, and give them what they want. If we don't *get* that information, we can't create a message that lands with them. So we have to build *trust* and *rapport* with our clients, so that they can reveal their most raw painful parts (remember; pain is important) and their truest desires. These are what we want.

"Well yeah, I ask questions. I try to figure out what's going on with the customer." **But before you even do that, you need to pay respect to that other human being**. Or they won't answer your questions truthfully.

Before we dive deeper, let's take a look at the human brain. This is important for understanding rapport. We all have what is called a critter brain. This is the old brain. We share it with all animals on this planet. The critter brain is looking for safety, "Am I going to live or am I going to die?" It doesn't care about quality of life. It only cares if you are alive. If there's a threat to your life, then it becomes that fight or flight. Notice, as you imagine something that could potentially go wrong, how your breathing changes and how your pulse rate increases. This is the critter brain operating. And even though we don't see it that prevalently in our life, it's still running. Our brain is checking if we're safe, all the time.

If a potential client is in the mode of fight or flight, this makes it hard for you to have an interaction with them. a potential client,. Imagine trying to serve a client who is either fighting you or running away? You can't. **You need to create safety and trust so they calm down,** and you can have a proper interaction. That's where building *rapport* comes in.

Rapport is when we're creating a connection with another human being which is also important for marketing—so what you learn in this chapter actually connects to previous chapters. If you don't have rapport it makes everything else 10 times harder, or even impossible, because you're going to have a disconnect with that other human being.

So how do you build rapport? How do you have such a great level of rapport with a person, so they become comfortable with you in the first meeting? Well, before we get into the answer, let's just say there are *many layers* to rapport. But I will share with you the **key layers** that will be useful for you to start with. If we tried to cover all of it, rapport would a whole book in itself. If you want to study more about rapport, you can. But for the purposes of *capturing clients* and *closing deals,* , we will cover 5 ways:

1. Mirroring and matching (physical)

2. Keyword backtracking

3. Voice volume

4. Voice tempo

5. Breathing

So let's start with the first one. If you're in the physical presence of someone, you want to mirror and match them. This tells the *critter* brain that you look and behave just like them. So it doesn't perceive you as a threat, because you look (physically) like someone they are familiar with, themselves! What happens subconsciously is the mind starts to see that you are just like them—like looking in the mirror. It actually puts them at ease.

For example: if they cross their legs, you cross your legs. If they cross their arms, you cross your arms. However they are sitting, or not sitting, take on their posture. If they are standing up, make sure you stand up or else there is a huge disconnect. It's like *yelling* at a child. If you stand up and look down on them, that is threatening So you have to match them at their level.

I have three children. I always have better conversations with my children when I sit on the floor like they do. Or, if they are lying down, then I lie down. If they're sitting on the couch, I sit on the couch. It builds a connection.

The other thing is, if you're in a fight or argument with someone, the first thing you want to do, to prevent the situation from escalating, is get in physical rapport by matching and mirroring them. Isn't that rude or mocking? Not at all. If your intention is to build trust, they will appreciate it. If you are purposely just mirroring and matching everything they do—just for the sake of that—it can be off-putting. **Intention matters.**

When you're in a sales engagement, it immediately puts a softness around it. It allows a space where you can ask more meaningful, deeper questions and have more peace with the person that you're with. Their guard starts to go down, which allows space for vulnerability. This is how you can get to their deepest desires and their deepest pains—we will explore this, in even greater depths, in the coming chapters. **So remember, the first step is to match and mirror so you have *physical* rapport.**

Okay, the second step is *keyword backtracking*. You can use it face to face or on the phone. Keyword backtracking is when you hear someone say something key. Something that is important. For example, in response to a question "What about this is important to you?" a client could say, "One of the most important things for me is that I have a corner office, and I can see out the window." You then respond by saying something like, "Okay, so having *a corner office* is important to you so that you can *see out the window.*" And they're going to say yes. It'll land perfectly with them.

They will feel heard and acknowledged. They will feel more at ease because you heard them, and used their words so their subconscious mind will think, "Oh! They're like me!" That creates safety and trust. Go back to the example about the wow client who says, "I want the color red." And then you say, "I have red." Now you've had a connection. They're like, "Yes, red." **But if I were to say *burgundy* because I like burgundy (a shade of red), I'm going to have less success because I didn't use the exact words that my wow client used.**

Developing this skill requires acute listening—this is developed over time. You want to pay attention and find the words that they are saying that are *important*, and backtrack it to them. That's why it's called *keyword* backtrack. To help myself, I take notes. I do this (take notes) each time I interact with a client—it's less than what I took years back—but I still take note of what they say. Because then I can accurately backtrack it to both my potential clients and my existing wow clients. **So remember to keyword backtrack. This is the second way to build rapport.**

Third, match their voice volume. So if someone is talking really loud, like I do, I tend to talk loud, or if they talk really soft, I talk really soft. As you can see, it is about matching them on an audio level. The same principle of matching or mirroring applies. And matching voice volume is especially important over the phone because you can't build rapport by matching or mirroring their body language.

Matching voice volume might be uncomfortable for you at first, because you are learning to talk at a volume that is different to what you are used too, but it will help you build more rapport with others. You want to actually start to find the way that they're talking and start to share that type of speaking style. So if they're talking really loud, then you want to raise your voice a little bit too. If you do this, you're going to be more in rapport (with your client—whether they are potential, wow, or both).

Fourth, match their voice tempo. This is where the *speed* at which you speak is important. If they're talking really, really, fast, then you want to speed up your talk. You want to speed up how you're saying things. If they talk really slow, then you want to slow down, and talk to them the way they're talking to you.

And last, is breathing. Match their breathing. Now what do I mean by that? If you notice they take deep breaths, take deep breaths. Or if they take shallow breaths, take in shallow breaths too. The first thing you want to pay attention to is how they breathe. Are they breathing into their chest? Or deep into their diaphragm? Is it through their mouth or through their nose? And how regularly do they take a breath? If you can breathe with them, on the same cycles or breathe like them, deeper or more shallow, you're going to connect with that human at a much deeper level. **This one is quite advanced and also very powerful. The breath communicates our state**. So the more you match it, the more they feel connected to you.

The more rapport you build, the more people will reveal their deepest pains and desires. You can connect with another human being on levels deeper than most people. This is a glimpse of five aspects of rapport—there are so many more. **But you should begin with these few**. One way you can quickly learn more rapport is to use flash cards. Make a flash card for your physical rapport. Make a flash card for your keyword backtracking. Make a flash card for your voice volume. Make a flash card for your voice tempo, the speed of your voice, and make a flash card for breathing. Then rotate them every day and focus on that *one skill* when you interact with everyone you meet that day; significant other, family, friends, colleagues, and clients. Don't try to learn all five at one time. Practice one at a time and see how that impacts your life—it will make a huge difference (**promise**)

In the following chapters, as you practice and deepen your rapport building skills, you will also learn more questions that will help you get to the heart of what your client is going through— their pain and their deepest desires. Like an onion, we are peeling the layers behind the same principles we have discussed throughout this book. The more layers we expose, the more you will be able to *capture clients* and *close deals* with more fun, ease and gratitude.

CHAPTER 10

Asking The Right Questions

"A quality life demands quality questions."
—Dr. John F. Demartini

I felt sick. I was on a detox to lose weight, and get more energy. But when I woke up that morning, my eyes were dark, I felt weak, and I wanted to puke. But a few days later, I was reborn! I had more energy than ever! I lost weight, got more focused and felt ready to take on the world! What am I getting at? You have to allow space for the unwanted pain. In detoxing, I let all the yucky stuff in my body come to rise, and clear through me. It felt horrible during, but afterwards, the results were **amazing**.

It's the same thing when we talk about people's pains. We need to let them surface for them to heal. If we don't (allow them to surface), they hold us back in business and in life. Many of us, as humans, we want to fix the pain point right away, so we meet someone or we know someone and they're in pain, and we tend to want to fix it immediately. **This actually doesn't serve the**

person; it's kind of like putting a Band-Aid on something instead of actually fixing it. The other problem is, when you treat them like a problem by trying to solve them, you reinforce the war they are having with themselves. We don't want that. We simply want to allow space for the unwanted.

In this chapter, we are going to explore our clients' pain in more depth. We are also going to *further* the discussion about asking questions (once you have a curious potential customer in front of you). Just like rapport, there are many layers. And the more layers we peel back, the more empowered you will feel in your business. So we will be asking questions to find answers to questions such as; "How do we start the conversation with potential clients?", "What are the questions that give us the info we need; what a client wants, what they need?" or "What do we want to invoke in our clients?"

Now, let's backtrack for a second and talk about what we have gone through up to this point.

Thus far, I've shown you how to:

- Pinpoint who your wow clients is

- Ask them what they want

- Use their response to create the right message

- Use *that message* (their words) to attract them in

Now, I have taught you to ask open-ended questions that are focused on *one* thing. Such as, "What's *one* thing you would like to achieve by the end of this call?" Or, rather than asking them how much they value our service on a scale of 1 to 10, we asked them,

"What is the greatest value that you gained from working with me?" Based on what your wow clients tell you from your survey, we create a message that uses their words to attract them. It could be through a networking event, speaking engagement, online ad, etc.

So there you are, in front of a potential wow client. You have them curious to talk to you—your audio logo worked (yeah!). You have a gut feeling they are a good fit.. So what's next?—your **strategy session**. A strategy session is what I call my meetings with potential clients. You can call these meetings what you'd like. When I do my strategy sessions, I am looking at whether the potential client is a good fit, where that potential client is in their business and life, where they want to go, and how I (with my magic token) am going to do everything I can to bridge that gap. Again, who are they? What's their *pain*? What do they have to *gain*? To get this specific information, you need to ask more questions.

How do you start the conversation?

The next step is finding out who you are talking to. This is just like making sure you have a *wow client*. We want to make sure the person you are speaking to is a *decision maker*. Or else it is a waste of time speaking with them. If they are not the decision maker, they *cannot* make the decision to improve their business. So don't waste your time (or theirs) by trying to help them improve their life.

Who is the decision maker?

You shouldn't ask that question directly. You want to ask something similar but much softer. You can ask, "Hey, I know it's early in the conversation, but if we were to work together—maybe we will, maybe we won't. We don't know yet. But if we were to work together, how would it work? How does your company make decisions?" Or you could say, "When it comes to your company's strategy, direction, budgets and spending, who is part of making those decisions? Can you tell me a little about that?" Alternatively, you could also say, "Assuming we work together, you are the one to decide that, is that correct?"

When you ask questions like these, one: it gives you the information you need, but, number two, it also allows the other person to share their significance and value. If they are the decision maker, they may pop their chest up. This can happen with men and women. It is not just men that do this. Women get empowered as well. So it helps them feel the significance that they have. This line of questioning also helps you determine who you are talking to (a decision maker or not) and what is going to be the next appropriate step. Because then, from thereon, the conversation will be based around, "Do I want to continue talking with this individual?" or, "Is my whole job to figure out who I am supposed to be talking to if this company is a fit?" Remember, if it is not the decision maker, you have to figure out a way to get to the decision maker. It changes the dynamic of the meeting. But if it is the decision maker, then you can go to the next steps, which is figuring out their pain, and how you can better serve your potential client's business. **So remember, find out if you are speaking to the decision maker.** That is the first step after getting them curious enough to speak with you.

The next thing, as you may have guessed, is you want to find their pain. We talked about this already and I want to bring it up, and go even more in depth than we had before. Sure, your survey and advertising might have dealt with a pain they have, and this (your advertising—your message) may have gotten them curious enough to speak with you. But now, you have an opportunity, if necessary, before they buy your product or service, to get into this potential client's *specific* pain. Remember, pain is a big deal and a lot of us, as humans, want to solve the problem right away. So you are looking at what you can do to solve the problem. But you can't just go off their surface answer. That's what got them curious, yes. But that *may not be the real problem.*

Here's an example: when someone says, "Hey, I don't have enough sales," and then we say, "Oh, you don't have enough sales. You know what? That's exactly what I do. I help people create more sales." Big mistake.

If you say this, you are trying to fix the problem before you identify the depth of the pain. Like I said in an earlier chapter, if your car broke down, every day for a month, and you are left stranded—not able to get to work, run errands, etc.—that is a problem. But the pain might be somewhere else. If you ask the question, "How does that affect you?" You will discover that it causes all sorts of issues. Such as, "I get yelled at by my boss at work, and I feel like I let my kids down because I can't pick them up from school, etc." **That's the real pain.**

So if someone were to say, "Hey, I'm not making enough sales," then the key question that I want you to ask is, "How does that affect you?" Then you just wait and listen. They might pause. Even if there is some dead air space, let that happen. **So often we are trying to fill silence**. You know what? Maybe no one has asked them this question in a long time; maybe no one has even cared to ask them this question. Their mind might be thinking about what is important. And then they might say, "Well, I'm working longer hours because my sales team is not doing what they should. I have to pick up more sales. So this is causing a bigger effect in my life because I'm working longer hours. I had to cancel my last vacation with my partner because I couldn't go. If I didn't stay, I would lose my job as a sales manager."

Now you are getting to something tender. So backtrack their keywords and dig deeper, "So you are canceling your last vacation with your partner, you are working longer hours to catch up and make sales yourself, and you don't want to lose your job as a sales manager. So how does that affect you? Then, they say something like, "My wife is really upset with me. We are fighting a lot lately. She definitely wanted to go on that vacation, and I am not home and present because I am working really long hours. It is affecting my relationship and then that makes me stressed out. I am not happy, Steve."

You see how this is going deeper and deeper? These are the areas where bonding with another human being will really allow you to know them; they will feel how much you care. Now, you are able to **really** help them because you understand the full extent of what is going on, and they are open to discuss these deep moments (because you've built rapport with them). You could even keep going deeper. "How is that affecting you?" This particular client responds with, "If I don't fix this soon I'm probably going down a road to getting a divorce—we are not in a good space right now." There is some urgency to fix something like this.

Unless we dig deeper, we aren't going to understand or know this. **Most of the time, we, as humans, do not share our deepest**

pains =If you really think about it, how often do we walk around in public with our heads down, sulking. Most of us do our best to kind of suck it up and hide all the bad feelings and thoughts we have. We put a smile on and go about our day. But the thing is, all our problems are really still there. They do not go away. So when you dig deeper to understand your clients' pain, know that you are not causing it. You are just bringing awareness to it, so that you can help them.

Let me explain it another way. Imagine having a file cabinet in your basement. In this cabinet, you store all those "bad" or painful memories—the ones you do not want to acknowledge or claim as part of you. You close and lock the file cabinet. You put carpet over it. Then, you carpet the whole basement, so you cannot hear (or see, or feel) any of these memories. You lock the basement down, and you go upstairs—never wanting to acknowledge these painful moments again.

So, when you are talking with a client (or a potential client), you are invoking the pain situations in people's lives—you are helping them re-open that buried cabinet—so that, with your help, they can start solving those painful issues they haven't addressed for a while. Because the fact is, just because we are ignoring those painful situations does not make them go away. More often than not, they drive major decisions we make in our life, without our awareness—this can cause big problems. **By you giving yourself permission to ask in-depth questions, to find the deepest pain someone is having, you are going to help them to make a decision to change their life.**

That is, if you are in integrity and you are doing what is right. If you truly can help them with what you are offering.

So, **question, question, question**—the key ones: "What is your biggest challenge right now?" and "How does that affect you?" Do this while building rapport with the 5 techniques I taught you in the earlier chapter. By understanding them on such deep level, you have an advantage. People do business with people they trust. If they buy you (i.e. if they trust in who you are and what you have to say), they will more likely buy what comes with you.

One time I was in Dallas, Texas and I entered a board room to talk to a potential client. (He was a Chief Marketing Officer— CMO.) Almost immediately, the gentleman says, "Go ahead and plug in. Show me what you got." It was a very macho environment. He figured I was going to be *presenting* like anybody else, since there I was walking in to help with his marketing.

I said, "You know what? I'm not sure if I'm going to plug in just yet." Right away he was like, "Oh yeah, you don't have anything to show me?" I said, "I'm planning *what* to show you, but I just don't know what's appropriate. I *first* need to know what's going on in your organization. What are the *current challenges* and what is it that you want, so that I can share with you what's best? So what's going to be most important?"

He agreed. From there we started going through his current marketing. Instead of my just accepting his saying, "Well, you see Steve, we just don't have enough sales," I went much deeper. By the end of the conversation, I discovered they had been given 12 months "to prove themselves." What I found out was, this was a newer department, inside of a billion-dollar company, and it was failing. They were losing hundreds of thousands of dollars in marketing and, two months before meeting me, he was given a 12-month ultimatum. If he did not come through with his sales targets, they were going to close the whole department. He and a group of other staff members would then be out of a job. And you can imagine what that meant for their personal lives; family, kids etc. This particular CMO didn't even tell his wife that he was going to lose his job (if he did not get his staff organized).

I was the first person in the organization, in his life, that he actually had this depth of a conversation with. For him, it was relieving—he was sitting there, owning all of that, trying to figure out how to solve the problem, all by himself. He was *too embarrassed* to share it with anybody else. He could not go tell the CEO because he did not want to be vulnerable and maybe get fired early. He did not want the staff to know because then they would freak. He did not even tell his wife because he was afraid of what she would think.

This happens to so many people. They wake up every day, look in the mirror and wonder if they can pull it off, feeling like they do not have any support. That is why it does not serve us to be that salesman or woman going out there pitching, and making offers before we find out the **real** situation that individual is in. **Remember, sales is about service and understanding**. We need to dig deep to find out what is really going on—what their pain is, and how it is affecting their lives.

During our meeting, he actually broke down and cried. Remember, I was telling you this was a very macho space; he was like a cowboy, a man's man. And he was breaking down in front of me. Because I was present with them, we become lifelong friends. I won the contract even though I was going up against much bigger companies. Other ad agencies that were going after the same project were much bigger than my company, but we got the job—

because I connected with that other human being. That man and I became friends; we even worked together when he moved on to another billion-dollar company. Because he trusted me, he bought from me again. **It is the relationship more than the transaction**. I will say that again; it is the *relationship more than the transaction.*

Many times I find that business owners and people out there, that are doing sales, are afraid of the pain because they want to take the potential client out of the pain immediately. Or, they are afraid that they are causing the pain—none of this is true. You are helping the individual become clear about their pain. You are helping them address their pain. Now, knowing the full depth of what is going on and their challenges, you are able to now help them in a much deeper, much more refined way, AND, as a result, help them create lasting and sustainable change.

We *want* to *get into their pain* and know what is really going on. By just using this one simple strategy, I have changed my conversion of clients from 1 out of 10, to 2 out of 3. Most of the time the third one is not a match by my choice.

You can do this too. Here's how:

In the recent example, with the CMO, everyone in his life did not even know what was really going on. So, if you want your client (or potential client) to reveal things that they have not shared with anyone else, you have to develop a deep connection.

Here's a suggested sequence of questions you can use to dive deep and explore:

- "What is it like to have _____ happen?

- "Tell me more about that ..."

- "What do mean specifically by that?"

- "Is there anything else affecting you?"

- "How else does this affect you?"

- "How is this affecting the people around you?"

- "What don't you like about that?"

- "How does that make you feel?"

- "How does that affect you and the people you love?"

- "Is there anything else that's challenging you right now?"

These are just examples of questions that you can use to dig deep. Keep asking until you get to the bottom of it all. Until they say "No ... nothing else." Usually, you are hitting this point when they say, "Well, there's one other thing." That "one other thing" tends to be the biggest, deepest, darkest secret that they probably did not intend to talk about. But, because you connected with them at the depth that you did, you were able to get to the deepest pains.

Remember, you're not creating the pain. It's already there—in a filing cabinet. Many times people will get into the conversation, but, when they sense that the client (or potential client) is experiencing pain, they'll change the subject—they feel like they're causing pain for the client. Not true.

When you can allow space, when you allow yourself to be present with someone as they go through those tender areas—pulling files out of the cabinet—they can let the pain pass. This process is transformational; it changes the way they see the situation. It changes their perspective. They realize what they thought they wanted is different to what they truly want. **You can actually help them move past the *real pain* they are feeling. Just like in a detox**.

But if we just operate at the surface level (and try to "fix"), more times than not, the pain comes back. Which then comes back to you, because they're like, "That didn't work. I thought that was going to make my life better."

So, turn to their pain; go deep. And remember, building rapport helps with this. Use **physical mirroring** to mirror their physical presence, use **keyword backtracking** to acknowledge that you are really listening, and sync up with their **voice volume** and **pace** as well as **breathing** to show that you are truly present with their pain. If you create a safe space where they can be with their pain, you will build rapport, you will *capture clients,* and you will *close deals*.

By doing this, you will grow your business. Everyone will look at you and say, "That's the man or woman that has helped me so much, they're the one that connected with me like no one else before!" So I want you to allow this space (for them to connect with their pain). And then, once you have that, you can go to their desired state—which is what we're going to talk about next.

When you get to this point, you then backtrack all their keywords (regarding their pain). That way you build rapport, as we discussed in the previous chapter.

So, in summary, after we explore the full depth of what is going on, in terms of their pain, backtrack their keywords, and allow space for the unwanted, we then ask, *"Okay, after having had this experience, what is it that you would like?"*

In the next section of the book, we will explore how we can get to the depth of their *desires*. **Once you address the pain, you can focus on the gain.** Again, it is all about digging.

PART SIX

Find Their
Deepest Desire

CHAPTER 11

Go Beyond The Surface

"The mind is like an iceberg,
it floats with one-seventh of its bulk above water."
—Sigmund Freud

They are in tears. They are in pain. You are holding space for the unwanted feelings. What next? That's what this chapter is about. Having connected with their pain, the key transition sentence is, "After having had this experience, this challenging experience that you're having, let's put that aside, what is it that you would like?"

In this chapter, we're opening up the door for finding out their hope, their freedom, their desires, and what is it that they *really* want. And, once again, we're going to want to dig deep. Here's an example: If someone said, "I want more sales." Then you can say, "Okay, you want more sales ..." **Notice that I keyword backtracked**. "... *And what will having that do for you?"* That's the magical question. "What *will* having that do for you?" Years back,

I had a particular client that was earning 7-figures a year. Basically, he was a millionaire. He would hire me, privately, to teach him the same award winning approaches—to *capture clients* and *close deals*—that I teach to thousands in my *Design It* course—.

So this particular individual, even though he was earning 7-figures, said, "I want more money." So I asked, "So you want more money. What will having that do for you?" He pauses. Thinks for a while and then responds, "I want to be able to hire more staff and have more free time. I want to do more things with my family." **That's *very* different to "I want more money."** That's what *one question* can do. We call this *chunking up*. *Chunking up* helps someone get really deep into their desires.

But it doesn't stop there. You can ask the same question more than once. "And what will having *that* do for you?" No different to the previous question in an earlier chapter, "How does that affect you." But, this time, we are focusing on their *desires*, not their pain.

So let's suppose we continue with the previous example. "So you will be able to hire more staff, have more free time, and you will do more things with your family … and what will having that do for you?" He pauses and *really* thinks about it. "I can resurrect things with my wife, because I haven't been able to spend as much time with her." That's just asking the same question one more time. With enough rapport, we can ask the *same* question again. "What will having that do for you?" He responds, "Then we can have time off together, and go on a couple of vacations. We will be a lot happier too."

In this particular instance, I can see his face light up. So I sum it up by **back-tracking** his phrases. "So when you have more money, you will be able to hire more staff, have more time with your family, you will be able to go on a couple more vacations, *and* be a lot happier too. Did I get that all right?" His response, "yes." The other question you can ask, at the end of the previous one, is "Is there anything else that you would want?" It just helps clarify their desires.

Think about it: if we stop at just "I want more money," we will find it hard to get to their deepest desires. In this particular instance, it was **what more money meant for his life**. But what he really wanted, ultimately, was to take time off to go on a couple of vacations and be happy.

Now, I know that he's going to be able to hire more staff. He will then have more time to go home early, spend time with his family, and take a vacation with his wife. That will give him more happiness. We are getting to the *feeling* of what he wants. Not just the surface wants. Then I can connect with him by providing solutions that will help him reach his desires. For example, "You know, I was able to help systemize increasing sales for many business owners, which has given them more free time to spend with their families, re-build relationships with spouses, and also take more vacations. Some of them, within the calendar year, were able to double, triple and sometimes even quadruple their revenue. But it's all based on the action that the company takes. I can give you all the golden nuggets (or tokens!), but you have to take action with it."

Now I have shared how I can help him, and so I also laid out my condition—"You have to take action." It is so important to set the right expectations. If I make a promise of how I can help, and the clients don't take action—nothing happens. It is a team approach. But, back to connecting a client with their deepest desires. Now that I have connected my client to his deepest desires, and I backtracked it, he will agree to my terms. So he says, "Yes, I understand."

Now, the conversation won't always go as perfectly as you would like. So you need to be armed with different questions so you can helpfully guide your client to their deepest desires. Here are some of the key questions and commands that will help you clarify what their deepest desires are:

- "What would you like?"
- "What is one thing you would like right now?"
- "What is one thing you would like to work on first?"
- What will having that do for you?"
- "Tell me more about that ..."
- "Anything else?"
- "What do you mean by that, specifically?"

All of them work together, and you can mix and match them—creating the perfect combination that suits both you and your client's needs. Let's discuss some of them (and in what context they are useful).

The last question, for example, "What do you mean by that, specifically?" is especially useful for people who are really *vague*. If they say, "I just want to feel better," what does better even mean? It could be going home early and sitting on the coach. Or, it could be going home to hug your partner. For others, it might mean getting some sunshine on the beach. By asking "What do you mean by that, specifically?" we can get a richer response.

On the other hand, you might have someone who is way too detailed, and gives you many things they want. "Oh I want a new car. I want to be able to take more vacations. I want to be able to have more freedom, more money, etc." Sometimes people give a laundry list of things. This is when you need to guide them to what's most important. . "Those are all good. Which one would you like to work on first?" Or you can ask, "What is *one* thing you would like?" This helps them narrow down their priorities. We need to help them decide on a single outcome. The more focused, the better. Just like a magnifying glass—if the sunlight is too focused, it can burn a hole in the paper. If it isn't focused, it just passes through, and only slightly warms things up.

The other key thing about getting their *desired* outcome, is making sure it is stated in the positive. Some people are just more negative in their way they talk and respond. If they say, "I just don't want to feel this pain anymore ..." You then ask them, "Hey—I understand you don't want to feel this pain anymore. Knowing what you don't want is important ... so what is it you would like?" You're just flipping the direction of their focus, so you can find out what they want.

Moving on. The other key thing I need to mention; you have to guide the flow of the meeting with questions. You don't want to *answer* their questions... yet. Remember, we are helping them clarify their desires. Some people will have questions, and try to change the flow of the conversation. A common question is, "How much do you cost?" Don't answer. If you answer, you lose the ability to control the meeting. So you have to divert the question, or put the question back to them.

For example, you would say, "Well that's exactly what I'm curious about. I want to know more about what's going on so I can best help you." The other way you can answer is, "Great. I won't be able to tell you until we actually further our discussion, understand exactly what you need, what you would like, and if we are a fit to work together. So tell me more, what is it would you like?" That puts you back in the power position to continue asking questions. Remember, you aren't manipulating. You are guiding them so they can focus on getting to their deepest desires. Or, if you are focusing on pain, you are helping them get there (towards focusing on their deepest desires) instead, as in the previous chapter.

I was just talking with one of my clients today. She was talking about how she had previously worked with a company where one of the heads of departments loved her, and hired her to do some work. Meanwhile, another head of department needed her, but they didn't see the value The other department said, "Oh, you're not for us ..." even though she clearly was, but the communication didn't happen. Now remember, I always say, there are only two things that can go wrong; **wrong person or wrong message**. What she missed out on, is what I'm teaching you here—*ask the right questions* so you can *get the information you need*. **Then**, use keyword backtracking to *communicate the right message*.

Here's the metaphor I used in an earlier chapter, and it's worth repeating: if someone is hanging off the cliff, and you know you can help them, and you say, "Grab my hand" and they say "No thank you." There is a disconnect in the way you are communicating. Clearly both of you want them (whoever is hanging from the cliff!) to be safe and sound. If you ask the question, "what would you like?" They might say, "I want a rope so I can get back up and be safe." And you can respond, "Oh, so you want a rope so you can get back up and be safe." It will connect with them. Using just *language* and *questioning*, that particular client of mine got a *second chance* to discuss her work to the other head of department—she got them to see the value.

Now, to further clarify what the client wants, there are *other variations* to the questions we have covered thus far. For example, you can say:

- "If you picture having what you want right now, what would that be like?"

- "So there you are, having what you want, what would that be like?"

- "How will you know when you have that?"

- "When would you like it?"

- "Where and with whom would you like it?"

This helps them arrive at greater clarity, as well as connect more, emotionally, with what they want.. You want them to connect with the *emotion* of having what they want. By using these questions, you can get a sense of what they are *looking for*—the real world experiences, images, pictures, sounds and feelings that *represent* what they really want. It makes their desired outcome *richer* and adds more *context*.

Then, when we think we have gotten as rich a response as we can from the client, we ask them "Did I get it all? Is that everything you would like?" Again, they are likely to say yes. Then we can move on. And, at that point, you can say "Would you like me to help you with that?" This is an invitation for them to work with you. Now, most people will say, "Well I want your help but I'm not sure because I don't know how much it costs..." And then you can re-divert the question. You can say, "I understand. Assuming we do work together, and can agree on a cost, would you like me to help you with that?" Likely, they will say yes.

Then you say, "When would you like to have this?" And if you've done this really well, more times than not, they're going to say, "I want this right away." I've heard people say, "I want this yesterday, as soon as possible, tomorrow, quickly, in the next week please." You'll get answers like that. Some clients, organizational ones, say, ""In Q2, quarter two, we're going to be ready for that." But that's great. At least you know a timeframe. Then we start moving the potential client forward, and agreeing on a fee for service. This is called *making the match before you talk money*. This will be the focus of the next chapter.

PART SEVEN

Making The Offer
Simple With Integrity

CHAPTER 12

Make The Match
Before You Talk Money

*"There is a saying that every nice piece of work needs the
right person in the right place at the right time."*
—Benoit Mandelbrot

You're in service. Not selling. Whatever it is, even if you're entertaining someone, you are providing a service. Entertainment helps people de-stress. It helps them check out of a busy lifestyle for a while. So, in this chapter, we focus on *making the match* before you talk about the money. Part of that is realizing that what you have to offer is of *benefit* (**your magic token**) to someone. Once you know that, you can confidently ask the question, "Would you like me to help you with that?" Simple.

But as we mentioned in the last chapter, they might come back to you with many answers or questions *before* they can commit to a yes or no. What we want to do is help them *arrive* at either solution. We don't want to answer their question immediately, especially if it is about *costs* or *other details*. If you answer their questions too soon (esp. around cost), you don't allow yourself to clarify (and possibly disprove) any assumptions that they might be making about you or your business; they might be assuming something that is *not true* and make a decision *not* to work with you—which could result in a huge loss for them. You aren't going to work with everyone. It is not possible to serve *everyone* in the world (who is living and breathing as a client).

Or, as another example (of how you can't work with every single client in the world), I have a lot of different courses, so if someone wanted to work with me one on one and they couldn't afford to do that, then I would say, "Hey, come attend my *Design It* course. You're going to be able to boost your business and then maybe you can afford to hire me one on one or not." You can sell them into something else that works. Sometimes you might find that they're not ready for you and you need to recommend them to somebody else that can help them get to the next level before they can hire you. And that's fine too—they're going to always respect you for that. BUT, if you begin answering their questions too soon—allowing them to divert the conversation—you may not even get to this point. SO, **guide** them to the right solution.

Here's the awesome thing though—even if you don't work with them, they will remember you for the clarity you helped them achieve. That's the result of the strategy session. Or what you call a *clarity* session. Most people aren't given the opportunity to have someone build trust, ask questions, and really understand their deepest pains and desires. So if and when they have a need, down the road, even if they don't work with you immediately, they will *remember* you and likely contact you. They will also likely refer you to other clients.

Remember, you aren't in the business of a product or service. **You are in the business of moving and serving people**. We covered this in Chapter 1. So there you are, in front of your potential client. You have a clear sense of their desire, you know you *can* help them, and you have asked them the question, "Would you like my help?" **This is a key question**.

They likely won't say yes or no right away. If they say yes (right away), great. But, more often, they will share their thoughts, concerns or any additional information (they need) to make an informed decision. "Well, I don't know. I don't know how much you cost. I don't know how much this is going to cost." As discussed in the previous chapter and, we will continue here, you have to *guide them* with questioning, and refrain from giving them an immediate answer.

You can use words like, "You know what, I understand, and we'll get to the money, but I first need to know if it's exactly the amount of money that you can afford—would you like my help?"

If they say yes, good. But if they continue with other questions, concerns or thoughts, you have to keep things flowing. They might come back to you with, "Well I don't know enough about it yet." And you might say, "Great, we'll help you know enough soon. Assuming you do get all the information you need to know, would you want my help?" As you can see, this is where keyword backtracking is important. You use their words, "know enough," so you can move them to a space where they can actually answer *yes* or *no*.

And then, if they say yes, you proceed. If they say no, then there's no sense of proceeding. But what if they get angry with you for not answering their question? If you've built rapport, you are in a good space to handle any agitation that might surface—you can respectfully guide them back to their desires. If they insist on having their questions answered first, then it's just not a good fit. Additionally, asking questions and clarifying is logical. If they have concerns about money and details, they aren't focused on the outcome. You need to keep them engaged on their desires. The money and the details are things that need to be clarified after you agree that you would work together. If not, it is a waste of your time to go further.

CHAPTER 13

Negotiate For
The Right Terms

*"It's learning how to negotiate to keep both sides happy -
whether it's for a multi-million dollar contract or just which
show to watch on TV, that determines the quality and
enjoyment of our lives."*
—Leigh Steinberg

"**Y**es, I want your help." That's what your client has just
said. Then we can move on to the next step. This is
about negotiating terms. If the right terms can be
found, then it is inevitable that you will *close the deal.*

That's why you always want the customer, the client, to say, "Yes, I
want your help. Yes, I want your product." Then, you can start to
discuss the finances, and find a win-win to make it work. Typically,
you won't get a flat "no"—you've had such a nice conversation,
you really connected with that person's pain *and* desires.

Now, it becomes a negotiation. The first part of the negotiation is to be clear on your terms of working together. What do you need in order to be able to work with someone? Remember, you are only working with your *wow* clients. You want to set the right expectations. Here's an example: I have three things that are a must. And clients have to have all three to work with me or attend any of my courses (such as *Design It*). And I tell people this.

Number one: you have to have a dream or desire for more. If you don't have that, then there's probably no point (in working with me)—you aren't hiring me to keep you stuck. **Number two**: they must be willing to take action. If you're not going to take action, year after year is going to pass, and that dream is going to stay a dream. **Number three**: be coachable. If you do have a desire and you are going to take action, but you're going to do it your way, and you're not going to implement anything new that I teach you, then it's definitely not worth it for you—so don't hire me. Don't get coaching from me. Don't come to my course. It takes **all three** of those to win in what I do. Don't get me wrong, I love them the same, I just know it is not going to work. So why not be honest in the beginning? If we follow through on a deal, when I know it's not going to work, then they will be even more disappointed because they've spent money, but not gained any results. It is better to have a little disappointment now, tell them it is not a fit (maybe help them in another direction if you can) and let them go on their way.

So check in with yourself, what are the rules that you're going to live or die by with clients? Is it a certain time-frame? Do you need them to commit to giving you information? What about written confirmation? You need to set your terms. What is mandatory? Is it that they can't be 5 or more minutes late? Remember this is discovering a match. This is not making a sale. When it's a match, it's beautiful and everything works out. So I want to be realistic. I want to look at this and say, "Who's going to win if they work with me?" If somebody is going to lose by working with me, then it's a no deal. I don't want any of that to happen.

Not only is it bad for your reputation because they're probably going to go share it online, but it's bad for you and for them because it increases stress. If you're like me, and you care about people, you're going to be upset that it's not working. You're going to be upset that you're not able to help them the way you help other clients. And then they're going to be upset because they're not gaining results. They will direct their anger at you, and you both end up buying *a problem* rather than agreeing on a solution.

So when it doesn't fit, you don't make the offer. It's that simple.

Now, same thing applies for them—they might have non-negotiables too. For example, they might agree to your fee or cost. But they might not be able to pay immediately. I use this example because money is a common objection people have. But if there is a match, we can *negotiate* payment terms. They might say, "I can't afford to pay everything now." Then I ask them, "Well, can you pay it in three payments? Let's divide this up. Let's not let money get in the way of you having what you want." Often, this works. It helps them plan ahead. And it also means you can *help* your wow client!

However, if they are truly in a bad spot and can't afford to work with you now, you can't push it. Sometimes you can't. Some people just can't pay what you need, and you can't lower your price that much. It could simply be a *close* match, but not yet close enough. Perhaps you need to give them a more affordable alternative; whether that is another service or product you have to offer, or to refer them to a partner provider. Or perhaps, they need more time, and you need to ask them to secure a deposit, and then pay the rest at a later date. But again, that depends on what *your terms* are too.

There is always a win-win. The purpose is to make sure you are clear on your terms, and they are too. In the next chapter, we talk about *closing the deal*. Everything up to this point has been about *capturing clients*, in particular, your wow client. All that work needs to be done to arrive at this point!

CHAPTER 14

Finish The Deal

*"People actually like you to ask for a sale
because it shows you value their business."*
—John Caudwell

"Okay, *this is how I would help you achieve your goal. It's going to cost [insert amount]. Sign here, arrange for payment, and we can get started."* **That's how you finish the deal.** Of course, I would have your paperwork right there—ready to do the deal. When someone says yes, they are committed. **When the win-win arrangement has been made, you have to do the paperwork there and then.**

So many people slow down the deal instead. They say "Okay great. I'll write up a proposal and then we'll get back to you. And you can sign it and we'll get started." No! You're in the emotional wheel right there, you're with them and they are ready to make a deal. Sign the papers right there. The rule—all you have to do now is *ask for the business and do the deal*. Most people complicate or extend this process. Instead, just do it.

Sure, I understand, you might need to clarify the details in writing. Meantime, you just need to have a generic form they can sign. And then all the details, that are specific to that person, can be added in when you're already working together. So have the pen and paper right there, and walk them through the *closing* process, "Put your name here. Put your address here. Put your phone number here. Put your credit card here." Even if you're doing it online, or on the phone, send them a link to your website, or PayPal, and *close the deal*.

Don't assume that they're going to do it. You might hang up the phone, and then they get distracted by their kids, text messages and emails. And the next time you call to process the form, they may have forgotten by then "Oh yeah, why was I going to do that?

Don't be afraid to close the deal and process payment. If you followed the steps as I have outlined, to this point in the book, you know you are helping people and they want to work with you. They want to know how to get it done. They want you to walk them through it. And if you are helping them, you deserve to get paid. If you are doing it for free, you aren't being fair to yourself or people in your life. This goes away from what we discussed in the last chapter—finding the win-win. You've already negotiated the best terms that work for both of you. **Finish the deal**. On top of that, for me, if they don't pay, they don't get their course or coaching. I have myself to feed, a family to feed and staff to care for too. Basically, if your client does not pay, you will not be able to do what you do. You'd have to go get another job, and maybe, just maybe, you'd be able to do this on the side as a hobby. How many people can you really help that way? Can you help them as effectively? Can you truly focus on helping people, if you also have to find a way to survive?

Getting paid for my value allows me to continue serving clients in the market. Think about it, if the oxygen pressure drops in an airline, who is the first person you are supposed to put the air mask on? Yourself. You're putting it on you first so that you can breathe, and then you can help other people. If you put it on other people, before you put it on yourself, you won't be able to help *that many people or anyone at all.* So *close the deal.* If you have followed the steps thus far, closing the deal is simply called *being fair.*

"Well, call me next week. I need to think about it." That's right, they might not say yes (they might not sign and pay immediately). This sets off alarm bells for me. If they say yes, but hesitate (like delay their final decision), they aren't committing to one my terms—you must **take action.** So I tell them "You know the people that enroll right away are the ones that typically take action. By taking action today, you are showing me that you will make this happen." Truly, I have noticed that those who enroll in my courses or coaching, on the spot, have a much higher rate of success. **How clients show up in this moment is typically how they will show up when they are making other decisions.**

Remind them of the goal that they have. Remind them of their urgency. They also just told you they are ready to do the deal. That means they ought to be committed. **People that say yes and take action are the ones that you want to work**—they're the ones that are going to get the results. They're the ones that are going to use your product; they're the ones that are going to use your service; they're the ones that are going to take what you teach them and go do it. So, when people delay, I start to re-assess whether they are the right wow client for me now.

For example, if I sense that a client is currently having issues with following through and/or commitment, I tell them <u>not</u> to take my *Design It* workshop. I tell them <u>not to sign up for my coaching</u>. I don't want those people that are sitting on the fence. They bring the vibe down. It's not that I don't love them. I love them equally. It's just that it's not a fit right now.

But we want to make sure we get them to commit as much as possible. Especially since you know the value and difference you can make to someone's life—you aren't doing them justice by delaying things. Remember the Texas gentleman I told you about? If he didn't perform in 10 months, he was going to lose his job (maybe even his wife).

He was the manly-man client who cried (the first time we met). He was ready to do business. Once we got clear on how to work together, we did the deal then and there. We didn't delay. If he said, "Let's talk next week," then the clarity and momentum would have dissipated. If you set another meeting, you have to remember where you left off, and that takes a lot of work. You have to revisit almost everything. You lose momentum. Which means it can stop you from making a difference sooner.

Now, I'm not saying "delaying" the agreement never happens to me. There are exceptions. For example, in the corporate world, if there is a board of advisors, it's a little bit more difficult to close on the spot—there is follow up involved. There might be more than one key decision maker. But you want to explore all avenues, for getting a commitment, then and there.

In some cases, clients might truly not be ready—this is fine. I met with a potential client once. He said, "Yeah, we'll get back to you." He didn't want to take action that day. I let him off. I didn't follow up. I carried on to the next person who might be ready to take action now. Maybe I'll follow up once or twice, but my goal really is to not even have to follow up—the decision is best made in the moment. Those clients, the ones that make a decision on the spot, are the people I want to work with. If you make a decision in the same day that I'm with you, I am excited. I know you're going to get stuff done.

Remember the client who said he'd "get back" to me? He did. About nine months later, he messaged me and said, "We're ready" (completely out of the blue). I didn't expect this, but it was a pleasant surprise. So we worked together, and, like I said, it was a nice bonus (a pleasant surprise). I don't chase or spend time on people who aren't *ready* to take action. I just carry on and find my wow clients who are ready now. But what I want to say here is sometimes clients that aren't your wow clients now, become your wow clients later. Let them come around on their own, when it is right for them. You focus on the people that are ready. Remember, it is about finding a match. And that's what we want, right? You don't want people to buy your product and put it on the shelf. I mean maybe you made a buck or two or maybe you made 10 or 100 or 1,000, etc. But, whatever you made, it will be short lived—if nobody uses your product, no one is going to talk about it. No one is going to refer people. It isn't going to lead to business growth.

You want your wow clients. You want the ones that are going to use your service or product because there is a chance they are going to go and brag about you. They're going to be your biggest followers (and fans); they'll brag about you on Yelp, Facebook, Instagram, etc.—telling all their friends about your amazing product or service, and introducing you to other people. They love you because you love them, and because your product or service helped them.

So what's the lesson learned? *Close the deal.* You want to work with clients that take action right away. *Close the deal.* And, unless you're not the right fit for them, or you have said the wrong thing, it should be a no brainer (especially since you have already agreed to the terms of engagement—previous chapter). **Remember, only one of two things could go wrong; wrong client, or wrong message**. If you follow each step (that I have taught you), I **guarantee** that you will *close deals* with clients that you love, absolutely adore. AND, not only will you earn more money, but you'll also help more people (while increasing your income), **guaranteed**.

PART EIGHT

Taking Action

CHAPTER 15

Success Does Not
Feel Normal

"Success is not final, failure is not fatal:
it is the courage to continue that counts."
—Winston Churchill

There was this little boy and his mom and they were walking hand in hand to the pet store. They were going in just to get some dog food for their dog. As the little boy walked towards the dog food section, he noticed a little fish in its fish bowl. And he said, "Mom, mom, I want this fish!" His mom replied, "No, we're not here for the fish. We're here for the dog food. Let's get the dog food and let's leave."

The little boy pleaded, "No mom, you don't understand, I really, really want the fish. Please, please, can I have the fish?" And the mom said, "No, we're not getting a fish today honey." And the little boy persisted, "Mom please can I have the fish. Please,

please, please." The mom looked at her sweet little boy's eyes and said, "Okay listen, if I get you this fish, you have to promise to feed it every day. Then, once a week, every seven days, you're going to have to clean the bowl."

"I promise mom, I'll do it. I'll clean the bowl and I'll feed the fish every day." The boy smiled and nodded enthusiastically. So his mom bought the fish. After the first week went by, the boy did what he promised he would. He fed the fish every day. On the 7th day, his mom said "Okay son, you have to clean the bowl now." The boy said, "Okay mom." So the mom took the boy into the bathroom, filled the tub with water, and they moved the fish into the tub so they could clean the bowl. The mom showed the boy how to clean the bowl, so he could do it himself in the following weeks. After she did that, she left him in the bathroom.

Not a minute went by and the boy ran out and said, "Mom, mom the fish. Mom, the fish." And the mom started running back to the bathroom thinking he must have pulled the plug or broken something. She ran in there and the tub was full of water, the plug was still there, nothing was broken and the fish was swimming in circle. And the mom said, "What's wrong son? The fish is right there." He said, "Yeah mom, but something is wrong. **The fish has all this water and it's just swimming in a circle.**"

His mom smiled and said "I see son. You see, that fish only knows that bowl. So even though there's all that water, he's just swimming in circle because all it knows is the bowl." **Does this remind you of anything?**

That's what happens when most of us want to change our business and life for the better. That fish gives us insight into human nature. You see, **many of us are in our own fish bowl—** own comfort zone—because that is what we are familiar with. Here's the problem: we are in a *clear fish bowl.* So we swim around, and every time we go around the bowl, we say "Oh there is what I want." We swim around again. "I want that." We swim around again. "I want that." We swim around again. "I want that."

Then one day we get the courage to jump out of the bowl, and venture into open water. But notice it doesn't feel normal. *Success doesn't feel normal.* Think about it, how are you supposed to know how that feels? If you've never been there, how do you know how it feels? You don't. So this success that you're seeking doesn't feel normal. Think about it. The first time you went on a date, the first time you rode a bike, the first time you kissed your partner, or, if you're a parent, the first time you held your child. It didn't feel normal. It can feel exciting, scary, stressful and even great, but definitely not *normal.* Definitely not something you've felt before.

Success, as exciting as it is, can feel scary. It's scary because, when you jump out of the bowl, all your friends and family, all of the people in society, everyone around you, they are going to warn you and say, "Hey! Get back in the bowl! You are going to die!" Or "Oh my gosh—you jumped out of the bowl. What are you going to do now?" They will tell everyone to convince you to come back to the bowl. Not because they don't want you to be successful, but because you are going to a zone that *they aren't familiar* with. So they will think you are in danger.

They're not deliberately trying to hold you back. They actually want you to be successful, but they are in the bowl too. They're sitting in the bowl and they have no idea what's out there. They don't know, so they are trying to protecting you. They're telling you, "Get back in the bowl, you're going to die." They actually believe that. But you have to watch who you choose to take advice from.

As an example: some people, that have less financial success than me, have tried to give me financial advice. I don't take it. How many of you have those friends that try to give you financial advice? It happens all the time. You have to watch who you choose to take advice from. **That is why you have to have mentors who aren't in your fish bowl.** Whether you hire a coach privately, or attend an interactive workshop, you want to learn from people who have been where you want to go. People who can **guide** you, as you transition *out* of that small fish bowl, to a larger fish bowl. **You need *new* fish to swim with.** Fish that have swam these waters before.

In the next chapter, I will talk about taking small steps to win. After you decide to make a leap (out of your comfort zone—your small fish bowl) for your **big** goals, you need to take **consistent action** to bring them to life. You need to *get comfortable* with the *uncomfortable*.

CHAPTER 16

Small Steps To Win

*"Be faithful in small things because
it is in them that your strength lies."*
—Mother Teresa

I was exercising to lose weight. Instead, I lost my ability to walk properly. You see, when I was heavy, I tried to make a big impact too fast. I'd lift too much weight and—pushing myself too far. It mostly hit my lower back. The extra weight, that I was carrying, mixed with over-doing it, tightened my back too much—there were some days I couldn't walk. I couldn't get in and out of my car, or show up to meetings. It was the opposite of getting healthy and gaining energy. And eventually, it put me out of action. I'd even gained more weight, and had to start over again (in an even worse position). That was a real bummer. So in this chapter, I am sharing the importance about taking action, but *chunking* it down to manageable and realistic steps. If you don't "chunk it", you will end up treading water, or, worse than that, two steps behind from where you originally began. So how does *chunking* it down relate to *capturing more clients* and *closing more deals*? I'm glad you asked (well, actually, I asked—but I'm glad you are still with me (reading)—we are almost to the end).

So many of us have our **big** dreams and **big** goals—that's great. You want to have your annual goal or two-year goal; it's this kind of thinking—setting a long term goal—that helps you think **bigger** . But don't spend too much time beyond that—things can change very rapidly, and you don't want to be so hyper-focused (on one single goal) that you become blind to what is happening (right in front of you)So once you have that one or two-year goal, you want to break it down into **small actionable steps**.

So how do we do that? We take our one-year goal and we divide it by 12, that's it. You're looking at 12 chunk sizes instead of one. Rather than trying to stuff a whole meal in your mouth, you are taking 12 portions and spreading it out over time. If it is a personal objective for example, such as buying a house, ask yourself, "How much is it going to cost to have that new house?" "How much do I have to make and set aside, within 12 months, to be able to buy that house?" Or it could be a vacation.

But it doesn't stop there. You can break the months into weeks. So rather than looking at what you have to do in a month, you look at what you have to do week to week. So you divide the 12 monthly chunks, into weekly goals. Now you have a clearer plan. You are now asking the question, "What do I have to do, each week, so that I can make the monthly goal?" You look at each week, and it becomes palatable.

Wait. We don't stop there! We have got to take it down and chunk it into *daily actions*. Then you can plan your day "What time do I need to wake up?" "Which days do I want to work and which days do I want off?" Suppose it is five days. Then you have to break the *weekly* goals into 5 daily chunks. By then, you can look at what you have to do and say to yourself, "Hey! I can do that." Or if you chunk it down and, if it looks unrealistic, you have to ask yourself "Okay. I need to take a look at my goal again and figure out how to leverage my time, work more per week, *or* extend the time-line."

Here's more specific *business example*. If I told you that, to get the *number* of clients you want in a year, you have to make *1,440 new business connections* that would be a lot, right? When I speak on stage, or run my *Design It* course, participants in the audience normally *nod* and say "Yes, that's a lot!" I say to them, "Well guess what? What happens if we divide that by 12? How many new business connections do I have to make?" Someone always answers and says, "120 new connections a month." Most the crowd agrees. So I ask them, "By a show of hands who thinks 120 new connections a month is still *pretty big*?" Most people put their hands up. "That's a lot!" they say.

"We're not done yet." I tell them. "What if we broke it down *further*? What if we made it into *weekly* chunks by dividing it by 4?" Of course, the answer is 30 new connections a week. As I look at the audience sitting, I notice a lot of them take a deep breath and sign in relief. Their body language tells me they are more relaxed. Some of them are already lighting up. After all, this means if you make 30 connections a week, that's 1,440 people in a year. I can tell people in the audience are thinking, "Yes, I could do that." But not all of them—so I don't stop there. I say, "What if we divided it, by, say, 5 working days? How many connections do you have to make a day?"

It's obvious. That's 6 new connections a day. Now it feels even smaller. People can say, "Hey, that's totally doable." Now, I'll cover more of this in the next chapter on *owning your calendar*. But let's suppose you only need to start with a *10*-minute call. Let's assume you have your audio logo and messaging right and you know what questions to ask. When you have this in place, you only need *10 minutes* to figure out if the person you are speaking to matches your *wow client profile*. That means you only need to spend *60 minutes* (an hour) a day to build your business! I promise you it will make an impact. It will drop your stress levels; you will gain confidence and clarity.

But to do this, you must *first put to action* the processes I have shared with you earlier in this book. **Remember, you have to define your wow client, survey them, and determine what *messaging* they need in order to get them curious.** Only one thing can go wrong on a call then. You have the *wrong client*— which is perfect! You will know *exactly* whether you should spend more time on them or not.

So, apply the same chunking principle to all the activities you need to have in place to *capture* your *wow clients* and *close deals*. That is— identifying your wow client and describing them in detail, surveying 6 to 12 of them and identifying their common pains, wants, needs and verbiage, and creating the *audio logo* to connect your message to the market. You can do this either with social media, networking, referrals etc. Then you ask yourself, how many *wow clients* do I need to connect with, in 12 months, to reach my *one-year* business goal? Then use the following:

- Chunk it into months by dividing by 12.

- Chunk it into weeks by dividing by 4.

- Chunk it into days by dividing it by the number of days you want to work on your business. It could be dividing by 5, for example, which is a standard work week.

Now you have a plan. In that moment, you now have a daily action plan. It's that simple. Will everything go *exactly* to plan? No. But you *have* to have a plan, knowing that things won't always go perfectly.. But if you don't have a plan, *nothing* happens. That's the paradox of it.

From there, once you have your plan, start executing it. And for wow clients that want to move to the next steps, after expressing curiosity, use the *process* I taught you in Section Five and Six of this book to dig deep into their pain and desires; then, once you've held space for them to dig deep, invite them to *commit* to buying your service or product. This part takes a bit more time. But again, once you notice *how many* wow clients you connect with, and how many typically end up *buying* and saying *yes* to your offer, you can use the *same* chunking principles to determine how much time you need to spend a week to *capture more clients* and *close deals*.

You might even leverage your time by using automated sales funnels, assistants or sales representatives. But that depends on what your business is. All these principles and much more than what I've shared here, in *Capture Clients Close Deals*, are the same that I share in my *Design It* course. I teach people how to use my principles *specifically* for their business, so they can earn more money, enjoy what they love, and live the life they have always wanted.

If your initial plan doesn't work, that's okay, you get a chance to reset or revise it. You get to start over, day after day. Dust yourself off and try it again. You can make changes by evaluating what worked, what didn't and how it can be better. "Okay, what I did today didn't work, so I'll make a different plan for tomorrow." That's what you want to say to yourself. Take 5 or 10 minutes at the end of every day and reflect on what happened, so you can make tomorrow better. So remember: *chunk* out your day, *chunk* out your weeks, *chunk* out your months—this will get you towards your yearly goal.

I want to share a metaphor with you. A bird flies by a yard and drops a seed on the ground. The bird makes sure the seeds are in the soil, and no other animal disturbs it. Over time, the soil and the seed get water and sunlight, and, eventually, becomes this great fruit tree—one that provides shelter and food for the birds. Here's the problem: it's only *one* tree. What if something happens to that tree? Does that tree provide enough for you to sustain? Most likely not. This is the same thing with your business—by planting many seeds, by connecting with your many wow clients, you don't just rely on getting one or a few. You cultivate a whole farm. You plant many seeds. If you talk to any farmer, they will tell you the more seeds you plant the higher chance of a larger yield.

So this is called farming, you have to go out and do this. You have to go plant seeds. So, pick an amount of time that is worthwhile (and realistic for your timeline), and plant, plant, plant.

As I said at the very start of this book, I'm giving you my all. And I've put a lot of great things out there for you so that you can take action and start *capturing clients* and *closing deals* without convincing or manipulating people. It is all about being of service; remember: you have the magic token. But you need to take action. You have to do something. You've spent all this time reading this book; now, DO something! If you weren't meant for greatness, bigger and better things, you wouldn't have made it this far, get out there—**take action**. *Knowing* does not mean *doing*.

To implement what I shared in this book, I suggest you *chunk* one or two hours on your calendar, and just start! Even it takes you two, three, four weeks to get through some of the activities, by the end of this month, you're going to have a much deeper understanding of what needs to happen to *capture more clients* and *close more deals*.

In the next chapter, I will share simple tips on what you can do to own your calenda—if you don't control your time, other people and other experiences will. You don't want to live a life and build a business by chance. **You want to succeed by choice.**

CHAPTER 17

Own Your Calendar

"Your time is limited,
so don't waste it living someone else's life."
—Steve Jobs

"Yep, okay, I'll do it." That's what I hear many people say after a meeting. But before they leave, I ask them, "Okay, when, specifically, you are going to have it done?" They pause, they think about it. Then they give me their answer. More often than not, I know this will help them get it done. Because, until they set a time, I know it won't get done. They will walk out of the meeting and probably forget about it altogether. But, once they set a time, they have to think about where the activity fits in their schedule before giving me an answer. They have it clear in their minds.

I do this for people I work with. I do this for myself. You need to know what you are going to do (as we covered in *small steps to win*) and when, specifically, you are going to do it. This chapter builds on the previous. It includes setting a time for everything that must be done for your whole year—when your vacations are going to happen, family time, business time, etc. For me, I want to have quality time with my family and build my business around that. So together, as a family, we *plan* our calendar for the year.

My family is the number one thing in my life—I build my business and my life around it.. I put my personal items on my calendar, like when am I going to be with my kids, when am I going to be with my wife, what I'm going to do on date night, etc. All of the things you want and love in life should go on your calendar—so you can own it. If you don't fill your time with things that matter to you, and get you closer to your goals, life will automatically just give you "stuff" to do and "stuff" to deal with.

A lot of people might say, "Oh that's horrible that you have to put your loved ones on your calendar to make it happen. If you love them, you wouldn't have to do that. You would do it anyway." Wrong. It's the exact opposite. Because I love them, I don't allow them to be replaced by something else on my calendar. I block out time for my family, on my calendar, and any business call or client need can be addressed during a different block (on my calendar). Without this, I see clients who don't have quality time with their spouses and families—because "something came up." That "something" is called bad planning. It's called *not* chunking. It's called being too lazy to take the effort to say, "No. I have to leave work now—I am taking my wife to a special dinner tonight. So I'd love to help, but we will have to book another time."

This leads me to another important point—you *don't* need your meetings to be as long as you think they should. If you have planned your meeting, and you chunked the activity down to *exactly* what you are going to address and talk about, you don't need it to be long. You also don't need it to be face to face. Some people like it because it makes them feel cozy or they think it is less effective (when it's not face to face). Wrong. If you have the right person to speak to, it's doesn't matter whether you are face to face or not, it's whether you are *saying the right thing*. This goes back to the core principle of the book—you either; have the **wrong person** or the **wrong message**.

When it comes to *capturing more clients* and *closing more deals*, these are the only *two things* that can go wrong. Back to my point: I see a lot of people looking for clients, spending hours at coffee meetings, having dinner, and traveling to meet face to face. But today, all that (searching) can be accomplished via a tele-call. You only need *10 minutes* to start. Start there. If it has to be longer, you will know *exactly why*. But don't make it longer than it has to be. When you place boundaries on the time you spend (on a call), you bring more focus to the meeting and your day. It's more efficient.

If you look at successful C level executives, or top entrepreneurs, they own their calendar and they are always strict with their time. They even have an assistant, who is great at scheduling, to help them manage and improve their calendar. For me, I do have an assistant, but I also leverage new technology. If you have an android or an iPhone, or any smartphone, you can use it to manage your calendar. If you plan your tomorrow today, you can set alarms on your phone so it tells you when to do what—"Beep, you got to do this. Beep, you got to do that. Beep, do this." It brings order and organization to your day. Anything that works to help you *own* your calendar is perfect.

Does it mean you *have* to be busy? No. You also need to plan your *breaks*. When are you going to have lunch? When will you meditate and relax a little? Take short and frequent breaks in between each activity. Go for a walk around your office; play (and bliss out to) some relaxing music. Some of my clients who play a musical instrument, such as a guitar, keep it in their office, and just play it for 5 or 10 minutes to reset.

Many of us run ourselves ragged thinking we have to get everything done back to back. But it is important to look at your life and look at when you're working at full power, half power or even less than that. Then decide when you give yourself rest time. Without energy, you can have all the time in the world you want. But you won't be able to use it.

How about emails? No. Checking emails is not a break. If you spend 10 minutes checking emails, that has to be calendared in too. You have to take a full break from *any* work activity. You need something you can do to *switch* off.

So, here are some tips for your calendar:

- Place all your personal things you want and must do.

- Place all your chunked activities for business and work there. Pepper in frequent breaks so you can relax and rejuvenate.

- Place basic necessities such as travel time, lunch time etc.

I can't tell you how many all-nighters I've pulled in my life, knowing that things weren't working as efficiently as I would have liked. Then I would get stuck trying to figure out something, but because I'm tired and stressed, I would end up just going to bed.

Why not fix that problem with planning? Owning your calendar allows you not to have that happen because you set blocks of time to get certain things done, and, because of this, you will have laser focus. You will get it done faster, and you will have breaks so you can continue to reset (so that you can maintain your laser focus).

In the next chapter, we will talk about tracking your results. How do you *know* you are doing the right things and that they are working out? It's important. Without tracking your goals, you won't know what needs to be *adjusted* (to stay on track).

CHAPTER 18

Track Your Goals

"Whenever I go on a ride, I'm always thinking of what's wrong with the thing and how it can be improved."
—Walt Disney

S
o there you are, you're driving on the road. Imagine that someone has covered your dashboard and navigator with a towel. How will that affect your driving? I imagine it would be pretty dangerous. You could be pulled over for speeding, run out of fuel, or you could end up driving in circles not knowing where exactly you are—this means that you won't be able to know, for sure, if you are getting to where you want to be.

So, here's the question: would you drive your car without a dashboard? Would you drive your car without knowing how fast you are going? And would you drive a car, on the interstate, without knowing specifically, how much oil there is in your car?

So why do it in your business? Same thing applies. It's a necessity to track what's going on; track your sales, track your calls, track your productivity (i.e. what are you getting done every day?)? *If you don't know where you are, you can't get to where you want to go.* I've had clients who didn't track how many calls or connections with potential clients they were making. They ended up dissatisfied with their results. And, as soon as we started tracking it, they were like, "Wow, I didn't make any calls that week, no wonder I didn't make any sales!" The next week, we made an adjustment to their calendar and activities, and surely enough they secured *five more clients* that week. They were back on track. That's the power of tracking. That's what I do for my own business, my private clients, and that's exactly what I teach during my *Design It* course. Tracking results helps you diagnose your problem, adjust, and *stay* on track.

For example, let's suppose that one of my clients started making calls. He might return and say, "Steve, I'm making the calls, but still haven't secured any clients." Let's suppose those calls were all *wow clients*. Then I know for sure he is saying the wrong thing. Why? Yup, you guessed it—it's either the **wrong person** or the **wrong message**. So I ask him, "Well, what were you saying?" For sure, he was *not* using the audio logo. Which is something everyone should have handy until the script becomes *natural* for you.

Remember: there are only two things that could go wrong, either it's not your perfect client, or you've got the wrong message. So you can reflect back and say, "Did I call the right people?" Yes or no? If it's a yes, then say, "I said the wrong thing." Now I need to focus on improving the words I say or the questions I ask. Adjust, and continue on. Keep tracking your success. Keep making improvements. This is huge!

Just remember, you need a *dashboard* for your business as much as you need a dashboard for your car. Get in the habit of making a scoreboard for yourself—track everything. It doesn't have to take a lot of time. You can track everything every day and then add it up, every week, and you can use things as easy as Microsoft Excel. There's other software that you can buy that does a more sophisticated job, but all you need is a simple spreadsheet. You just need to understand the basic principle. Once you understand it, you can find the technology to support you, or you can *hire* and *train* the right person to do it for you. It's a beautiful, beautiful, thing.

In this book, I've shared with you the core principles to *capture clients* and *close deals*. When you implement these principles, in the following days, weeks, months and years, you will be able to earn more money in your business *and* have the lifestyle you want. Or, if you want online support, to supplement your application of what you learned in this text, you can go online to www.ClientCaptureCourse.com and take the course.

If you are ready to *really accelerate* your business growth, and be held accountable to take the right actions, I strongly recommend my 3-day *Design It* course. I run it multiple times a year. It's not for the light-hearted. It's for the committed. It's for people who are ready to take action, get mentoring, and get things *done* (live—in person). People come from all over the world, as well as from all over the U.S., to take this course—Singapore, Australia, Canada, etc.—they fly to Northern California—where I live (to take my course). So why not just read this book (and not take the course)? Well, we go through *everything* in this book, and MUCH more in 3-days. People walk out with their chunked action plan—this includes all the core things they need to *capture more clients* and *close more deals*; **a wow client plan, an audio logo**, an **action plan** for your life and business, AND a tracking system that allows them to monitor all of their progress as they execute it—all of this *specifically* formulated for their unique business.

You can go to http://www.thenowacademy.com/courses/design-it/ to learn more and enroll. Or, if you know that this is not for you (right now or ever), BUT know of someone who would most definitely benefit from this course, please refer them.

Alternatively, if you know of someone who would love to attend with you, please reach out to them.

I will gift you a $1,200 contribution for their airfare and hotel. It helps them *save* on the cost of flying. Why do I do this? Because I know if anyone flies a long way, for the course, they are committed. And they are going to get results.

I have implemented ALL of these principles (that I've just shared with you) in my personal life. I've designed my life and business so I can be home with my family when I want, and take holidays to wherever we want. I have three kids and a wife. I get up, every day, grateful to be with my family, and to help people, just like you, have the life and business success that you want and deserve. My mission is to help as many people as possible have the freedom they desire in their life. If I can further help you, I'd be happy to do so. At a minimum, my heartfelt hope is that you **take action** with what you have learned in this book. When you take action, you get results. **I'd love to hear about them.** Connect on our social media, share and ask questions. My team and I will be there to answer back. With that said, I'll leave you for now.

With much love and gratitude,

-Steve

BONUSES

You can also **download the workbook accompaniment to this book at no charge here: CaptureClientsCloseDeals.com/bonuses**

You can learn more and/or enroll in the Client Capture Course here: clientcapturecourse.com

You can learn more and/or enroll in Design It here: http://www.thenowacademy.com/courses/design-it/

For more information on Steve Napolitan and/or to connect via social media, visit stevenapolitan.com

ABOUT THE AUTHOR

STEVEN **N**APOLITAN, a producer of award-winning content, has been recognized by national media as a pioneer in the online media market. He's known for designing campaigns that generate massive leads and high revenue. Here are just a few examples: the viral campaign for TaxBrain.com—"Stolen NASCAR," reached over 44 million, including 3 million unique visitors to their website in 3 weeks" Get More,", asocial media campaign for the City of Tracy's Auto Mall which resulted in 800 new car sales in a 10-week period, totaling over $19.2 million in revenue, and garnered 5.9 million impressions on Facebook with an average of 1,600 click-throughs a day to the campaigns promotional website.

Steve is an international #1 best-selling author. He's shared the stage with top speakers such as John Assaraf (star from the movie *The Secret*), Leigh Steinberg (the real-life Jerry Maguire—a billion dollar sports agent), John Maxwell (Author & Leadership Coach), Jeffrey Slayter (International Speakers & Human Potential Coach), Kane Minkus (Founder of the *Industry Rockstar Formula*), Loral Langemeier (Renowned Author/Speaker and Money Expert) and many more.

Steve has produced hundreds of advertising, marketing campaigns and internal promotions for many companies including Apple,

Intel, Charles Schwab and Nestle. He is a brand master, living and breathing brands throughout his work across all media types. He focuses on bridging the gap between a company's brand and their target markets by providing innovative marketing and communications with measurable effectiveness.

His executive coaching and training has publicly served over 45,000 professionals, business owners and entrepreneurs. Steve teaches professionals how to increase marketing/sales, while systemizing business to minimize their effort and maximize their revenue. Steve helps his clients have the lifestyles they desire.

Steve's branding and storytelling talent extends to films and television. One of his television series, *Livin Loud*, was picked-up by MTV for Primetime broadcast and, since then, has been sold to territories all around the world.

Steve teaches the *Client Capture* process, where he shows entrepreneurs how to grab the attention of the perfect client, while simultaneously leading them to the desired product or service in order to increase sales without convincing or chasing.

Ultimately, Steve is about people, relationships, and the convergence of vision, focus and teamwork that allows true freedom in life.

For more information about Steve Napolitan or to book him for your next event or media interview, please visit: http://www.stevenapolitan.com/speaking/

Made in the USA
San Bernardino, CA
27 October 2016